Jack the Ripper: A Solution

Karthik Sheshadri

December 23, 2024

Contents

1	Introduction	2
2	The Murders: A Grim Chronology	4
3	Literature in Ripperology	17
4	My Analysis	25
5	Known Suspects Through a New Lens	40
6	The Most Compelling Match	50
7	Final Thoughts: The Power of Primary Evidence	54

Chapter 1

Introduction

The mystery of Jack the Ripper remains one of the most studied cases in the history of crime, endlessly dissected and analyzed. Over the past 130 years, countless theories have emerged, each claiming to solve the riddle of the identity of the man responsible for terrorizing Whitechapel in the autumn of 1888. Yet despite the wealth of analysis and speculation, the case remains unsolved, buried beneath a mountain of conflicting ideas, conjecture, and interpretation.

For every theory, there is a counter-theory. For every story, there is a counter-story. The deeper I delve into the case, the more I find ourselves tangled in a web of contradictory views, leading to little progress. From straightforward suspects like Kosminski, a local Jewish immigrant with known mental health issues, to the more outlandish claims, like Bruce Robinson's assertion that a conspiracy of Freemasons shielded the true identity of the killer, the landscape of Ripperology has become a complex thicket of ideas, each leading us further away from clarity.

Indeed, a certain overlay of what one might even consider to be myth has built itself around Jack the Ripper. No better example of this exists than the movie starring Michael Caine, in which Robert Lees, Queen Victoria's fortune teller, pontificates: "Imagine two wheels turning, together but apart, like the wheels of a coach..look for a man with two faces". Well, really now, how's that for drama?

Given this rich background, it is natural to wonder what I, an amateur Ripperologist, uninitiated in the arcane lore that has formed around the case in internet forums, streaming websites, and geriatric gatherings over the last one hundred years may have to contribute.

My own approach to the problem is centered around a simple idea, which is that the evidence or observations that were made during or immediately after an event, have a much greater chance of conveying the truth than analysis, speculation, and "expert" opinion formed years later. My approach, therefore, draws a sharp contrast with Ripperology's speculative traditions. Instead of focusing on theories concocted decades or even a century after the fact, I return to the original events: the eyewitness testimony and observations made during or immediately after the events. To borrow a phrase from Arthur Conan Doyle, I should avoid the temptation to bend facts to fit theories and instead allow the facts to shape our understanding of the events. As time passes, the further I get from the events, the more difficult it becomes to sift fact from speculation, and the earliest insights tend to get buried in new theory.

While many Ripperologists have viewed the eyewitness accounts with skepticism, questioning the reliability of such testimony in general, questioning the accuracy or authenticity of the Ripper eyewitnesses in particular, and pointing out inconsistencies in what was observed by different witnesses, my perspective is different. I argue that, in fact, there is remarkable consistency to be found in these testimonies—if one knows how to look. Rather than dismiss the accounts for their inconsistencies, I embrace the possibility that each conveys a portion of the truth, while admittedly containing elements that are untrue. They align in ways that have been overlooked or misinterpreted by others. These accounts, collected close to the murders themselves, are far more credible than theories that Ire born long after the fact, often shaped by the biases of their authors. I use a data-driven approach to sift through this testimony, identifying common patterns from differing accounts, and using Artificial Intelligence to go from the initial descriptions of five or six different men, deeper into the story told by the eyewitnesses, watching in fascination as these several different individuals collapse into a consistent profile of one man.

It is my belief that Elizabeth Long saw Jack the Ripper. I also believe that George Hutchinson did, and that Matthew Packer did as well. And I believe that the data they have transmitted to us—though perhaps mildly obscured over years of retelling—combined with universal knowledge available through Artificial Intelligence, the FBI psychological profile of the man, and lastly, though less credibly, the Ripper correspondence (which may or may not have been from Jack himself), together conspire, almost mathematically, to paint a vivid picture of the man behind the knife. It may even go some way toward stripping away the mask that has confounded so many for so long.

To be clear, I do not claim to have solved the mystery of Jack the Ripper. Far from it. In fact, I recognize that the true identity of the Ripper may forever remain unknown, perhaps lost to time or buried beneath the relentless layers of speculation that have accumulated over the years. Personally, I believe the most likely truth is that Jack the Ripper was a local Whitechapel nobody, someone who lived among the residents of the East End, blending into the grim landscape of 19th-century London. A menial worker, someone who would not be looked at twice, someone who disappears into the background and is never considered, hiding in plain sight. However, the suspect I identify in this book emerges as the best of a bad choice, the second most likely solution, given the evidence available.

In the following chapters, I will build on the work of those who have come before us where applicable. While there is much to be said about the extensive literature on this case, I will resist the temptation to dive into endless rebuttals or derisive critiques of other authors. The case has been discussed so exhaustively that many key points have already been analyzed to death. However, when necessary, I will draw upon existing resources, and address some of the leading theories. Yet, I will consistently maintain a focus on what is closest to the murders—the eyewitness testimony.

The eyewitness reports have traditionally been met with doubt, falling into the trap of questioning the reliability of human memory or pointing out discrepancies between one description and the next. Instead of following this trend, I will show how a close reading of these testimonies reveals underlying patterns and consistencies that might guide us toward a clearer understanding of who Jack the Ripper really was.

Chapter 2

The Murders: A Grim Chronology

Accounts of the "Autumn of Terror" are available a dime a dozen on the internet. The present writer, however, is not thereby released from his obligation of providing descriptions of the murders here, to enable a self-contained analysis within this book.

The streets of Whitechapel, 1888, were a place of darkness, poverty, and violence. Life in this part of London was difficult for many of its inhabitants, particularly the women who lived hand-to-mouth, often resorting to prostitution to survive. Amidst this backdrop, a series of brutal murders took place that would send shockwaves through the community and across the world. These murders, attributed to an unknown killer who came to be known as Jack the Ripper, were distinguished not only by their savagery but by their apparent precision and purpose. This chapter provides a detailed account of the five canonical murders, which form the foundation of what became known as the Autumn of Terror.

Mary Ann "Polly" Nichols – August 31, 1888

The body of Mary Ann Nichols, known to her friends as Polly, was discovered in Buck's Row, Whitechapel, in the early hours of August 31, 1888. She was the first of what would come to be known as the canonical five victims of Jack the Ripper. Polly Nichols was a 43-year-old woman who had fallen on hard times. Like many women of the East End, she turned to prostitution to survive, relying on the meager income it provided to pay for her nightly lodging. On the night of her death, Polly had been turned away from her usual lodging house because she lacked the four pence required for a bed.

At approximately 3:40 AM, Charles Cross, a carman on his way to work, stumbled upon her body lying on the ground near the entrance to a stable yard. Initially, Cross believed Polly to be either drunk or unconscious. He later described seeing a bundle in the road, which upon closer inspection, he realized was a woman. Cross, However, was not alone for long. Another man, Robert Paul, arrived shortly after and found Cross standing by the body. The two men briefly discussed what to do. Paul touched her face and hands, remarking that she was still warm, but believed she was dead. Cross, who later claimed he didn't want to get involved, suggested they should go on and inform the first policeman they met, which they did.

Interestingly, there has been some confusion and suspicion surrounding Charles Cross, particularly around his name. When he gave his testimony, he referred to himself as Charles Cross, yet his real name was Charles Allen Lechmere. This discrepancy has led some modern investigators to question whether Cross may have had ulterior motives for not using his real name, and to speculate that his presence at the scene was more than coincidental. His timing and proximity to the scene of the crime, combined with the use of an alias, have made him a suspect in certain circles.

When Police Constable John Neil arrived at the scene, he found Polly's body lying on her back, with her skirts pulled up to her waist, exposing the lower part of her body. Her throat had been deeply slashed twice, and there Ire signs of blood pooling around her neck. However, Dr. Rees Llewellyn, the surgeon who was summoned to examine her, initially did not notice the more gruesome injuries to her abdomen.

Dr. Llewellyn later explained in his testimony: "I was called to Buck's Row, where I found the body of a woman lying on her back with her throat deeply cut. The incisions Ire so deep they nearly severed the head from the body. I examined the body quickly and found no other injuries at the time. I believed she had only been dead for about 30 minutes."

It was only during the post-mortem examination at the mortuary that Llewellyn discovered the mutilation to Polly's abdomen—the telltale sign that this was the work of the Ripper. Her stomach had been slashed open, though this detail had gone unnoticed in the darkness of Buck's Row.

There is some debate among modern Ripperologists about whether Polly's skirts were pulled down to cover the mutilations after the killer fled, or whether Charles Cross (Lechmere) himself may have done this upon finding her. In one version of events, it is suggested that the killer—likely disturbed before completing his work—pulled her skirts down to conceal the injuries in a hasty attempt to avoid detection. Others argue that Cross, trying to preserve some modesty for what he assumed was an unconscious or dying woman, pulled her skirts down before leaving to find help. This remains a point of contention, with no clear resolution.

Upon further examination at the mortuary, Dr. Llewellyn reported: "There were several slashes across the lower abdomen, and the intestines Ire visible through the wounds. The incisions were made with a sharp blade, roughly six to eight inches in length. Though crude in some respects, they demonstrated a degree of knowledge about the anatomy."

Llewellyn's delayed recognition of the abdominal mutilation is a significant detail. It highlights the chaotic nature of the early hours following the discovery of Polly's body. In the rush to assess the situation, the depth of the mutilations was overlooked, leading to the initial belief that this was a simple throat-slashing. However, as the pattern of mutilation became clearer in subsequent murders, Polly's case took on greater importance as the first known victim of Jack the Ripper.

The final element of mystery surrounding this first murder involves the time of death. Charles Cross claimed that Polly's body was warm to the touch, suggesting that she had died moments before he found her. However, Police Constable Neil, who had patrolled the area just 30 minutes prior, had not seen anything unusual. This narrow window of time raises questions about whether Cross may have arrived on the scene earlier than he claimed. Some theorists suggest that the killer may have still been present when Cross and Paul discovered Polly's body, possibly hiding in the shadows or escaping just moments before their arrival.

Polly's murder, though brutal, was relatively restrained compared to the horrors that would follow. Her death marked the beginning of a series of killings that would escalate in both violence and mutilation, but even in this early case, there Ire clues—some obvious, others subtle—pointing to the calculating, cold-blooded nature of her killer.

Annie Chapman – September 8, 1888

The second of the canonical five victims of Jack the Ripper was Annie Chapman, a 47-year-old woman who, like Polly Nichols, had fallen on hard times and turned to prostitution to survive. Her body was discovered in the early morning of September 8, 1888, in the backyard of 29 Hanbury Street, Spitalfields. Annie's murder showed a marked escalation in the brutality and mutilation compared to that of Polly Nichols.

Timeline of Events and Eyewitness Accounts

On the night of September 7, Annie Chapman was seen at a local pub called the Ten Bells, a notorious haunt of the poor and destitute of Whitechapel. Witnesses at the pub described Annie as being in poor health. She suffered from tuberculosis and was in a weakened state from years of drinking. Earlier that night, she had tried to get a bed at Crossingham's lodging house, where she was staying, but had been turned away because she lacked the money to pay.

Several eyewitnesses reported seeing Annie Chapman in the hours leading up to her murder:

Emily Walter : Around 2:00 AM, a woman resembling Annie was seen near the crime scene. This sighting is unconfirmed, but the witness described a man with a dark beard and a black felt hat— an ominous figure who could have been her murderer.

Elizabeth Long : At 5:30 AM, Elizabeth Long saw Annie talking with a man outside 29 Hanbury Street, just minutes before her death. She provided a detailed description of the man, noting his dark complexion, brown deerstalker hat, and possibly a dark overcoat. Long said that the man appeared to be over 40, somewhat taller than Chapman, and had the appearance of a foreigner. The two were standing close, and Annie appeared to be engaged in conversation with him. According to Long, she overheard the man ask, "Will you?" to which Annie replied, "Yes."

John Richardson: At 4:45 AM, John Richardson, a tenant at 29 Hanbury Street, sat on the steps of the yard to trim a piece of leather from his boot. He noticed nothing out of the ordinary at the time and did not see anyone in the yard. He would later provide testimony at the inquest but admitted he didn't look closely into the yard itself.

Albert Cadosch: At approximately 5:15 AM, Albert Cadosch, who lived next door at 27 Hanbury Street, heard voices and the sound of something falling against the fence that separated the two properties. Cadosch didn't investigate further and simply continued about his morning. This sound is now believed to have been Annie falling or being thrown against the fence during the attack.

Discovery of the Body

At approximately 6:00 AM, John Davis, another tenant of 29 Hanbury Street, discovered Annie's body lying on the ground in the backyard. He immediately raised the alarm, and the police were summoned. When they arrived, they found Annie Chapman lying on her back with her skirts pulled up, exposing her abdomen. Her head was tilted to one side, her eyes wide open, and her throat had been deeply slashed in two brutal cuts, severing her windpipe and spinal cord.

However, it was the condition of her abdomen that shocked the police and the attending medical examiner, Dr. George Bagster Phillips. Her intestines had been removed from her body and placed over her shoulder, and part of her uterus, bladder, and vagina had been cleanly excised and taken by the killer.

Dr. George Bagster Phillips conducted the post-mortem examination and later testified about the horrifying condition of Annie's body. He described the scene as one of brutal efficiency, noting that the abdominal mutilation was far worse than that inflicted on Polly Nichols.

Dr. Phillips remarked: "The abdomen had been entirely laid open. The intestines had been lifted out and placed on the right shoulder. A section of the uterus was missing, along with part of the bladder and vagina. The injuries Ire inflicted with considerable anatomical knowledge, as the organs Ire removed with precision."

Phillips believed that the killer had some experience in anatomy, either from medical training or through butchery: "This is not the work of an amateur. The manner in which the uterus was removed suggests that the killer knew where to cut. The incisions Ire clean and precise, requiring both skill and a sharp knife."

Annie's personal effects were found scattered near her body, including a piece of muslin, a comb, and a broken envelope containing two pills. Like Polly Nichols, there was no sign of robbery or sexual assault, indicating that the motive behind the murder was something far darker.

Theories and Interpretations of the Eyewitness Testimony

The conflicting descriptions of Annie's attacker provided by eyewitnesses have fueled speculation and debate for over a century. Elizabeth Long's testimony of seeing a man with a dark complexion, brown deerstalker hat, and dark overcoat stands out as one of the most detailed eyewitness accounts in the Ripper case. Her description of him as a foreigner and her noting that he was taller than Annie, who was only about 5'0", are significant. Some have speculated that the man Long saw could have been Jewish, fitting the general profile of Kosminski or other suspects with Eastern European backgrounds.

However, the accuracy of Long's account has been called into question by some researchers. She admitted that she only saw the man from behind and could not be certain of all the details. The timing of her sighting, just minutes before Annie's death, suggests that the man she saw may have been the killer, but this remains speculative.

John Richardson's presence in the yard just 15 minutes before the murder is also intriguing. Some have questioned how he failed to notice the killer or any disturbance, but it's likely that Annie and her killer entered the yard after Richardson left. His testimony, though brief, confirms that the yard was quiet shortly before the attack.

Finally, Albert Cadosch's account of hearing a body fall against the fence adds another layer of mystery. It's likely that this sound was Annie being thrown or falling during the attack, yet Cadosch did not investigate further, a fact that has frustrated both contemporary investigators and modern researchers alike.

Escalation in Mutilation and Precision

Annie Chapman's murder demonstrated a marked escalation in the violence and mutilation compared to Polly Nichols. The removal of organs and the surgical precision with which they Ire excised led investigators to believe that the killer had some form of anatomical knowledge. Dr. Phillips strongly believed that the killer was either a doctor or a butcher, though modern criminologists have suggested that such knowledge could have come from experience with animal slaughter.

The removal of the uterus, in particular, suggests that the killer was operating with some specific goal in mind. This has led to theories about the killer's motives, with some speculating that he may have been harvesting organs for sale on the black market, though no evidence has ever been found to support this theory.

Annie Chapman's murder also introduced the concept of the killer working in a private, enclosed space. Unlike Polly Nichols, who was killed on a public street, Annie was murdered in a backyard, out of view from passersby. This has led some to suggest that the killer was becoming more confident, taking greater risks by spending more time with his victim and performing more elaborate mutilations.

Annie Chapman's murder remains one of the most brutal and baffling in the Jack the Ripper case. The eyewitness accounts provided tantalizing glimpses of the killer, but the conflicting details have left investigators with more questions than answers. The escalation in the mutilation and the precision of the organ removal marked a turning point in the Ripper killings, cementing the killer's reputation as a methodical and sadistic murderer.

The case of Annie Chapman, with its grisly details and frustrating near-misses with eyewitnesses, continues to captivate Ripperologists and true crime enthusiasts alike. Her death, like those that followed, serves as a chilling reminder of the darkness that lurked in the shadows of Whitechapel during the Autumn of Terror.

Elizabeth Stride – September 30, 1888

Introduction

The murder of Elizabeth Stride, known as "Long Liz," presents a unique case in the Ripper murders. Unlike the other canonical victims, Stride's body was not subjected to the gruesome abdominal mutilations that Ire seen in the other murders. Many theorists believe this is because the killer was interrupted during the act. Stride, a Swedish-born woman in her 40s, was found dead in Dutfield's Yard, off Berner Street, in the early hours of September 30, 1888—the same night Catherine Eddowes was killed.

Timeline of Events and Eyewitness Accounts

Several witnesses saw Stride on the night of her murder, and the timeline surrounding her final hours is crucial in understanding what happened. Unlike some of the other Ripper victims, Stride was seen with multiple men that night, leading to some confusion over the identity of her killer.

J. Best and John Gardner

At 11:00 PM, J. Best and John Gardner, two men who knew Elizabeth Stride, saw her standing outside the Bricklayer's Arms pub on Settle Street, speaking with a man. They described him as being about 5'5", with a black moustache, and wearing a morning suit and bowler hat. Best and Gardner later testified that the man had an English appearance. According to them, Stride was reluctant to go with this man, and when they mocked him, the man became defensive, hurrying Stride away.

CHAPTER 2. THE MURDERS: A GRIM CHRONOLOGY

William Marshall

At 11:45 PM, William Marshall, a laborer living on Berner Street, saw Stride standing with another man near Dutfield's Yard. He described the man as middle-aged, stout, and about 5'6", with no moustache and wearing a black coat and round sailor's cap. Marshall heard the man give Stride a peck on the cheek and say, "You would say anything but your prayers." This somewhat intimate encounter has led to speculation that the man was the killer, though the tone of the interaction seemed casual and non-threatening.

Matthew Packer

Shortly after midnight, Matthew Packer, a fruit seller, claimed to have sold grapes to a man and woman, who he later identified as Elizabeth Stride and her killer. The man, according to Packer, was 5'7", between 25 and 30 years old, and dressed in a long black coat with a felt hat. Packer's story has been subject to scrutiny, as there is no conclusive evidence linking the grapes to the murder scene, but he maintained that Stride had been with a man in the moments leading up to her death.

P.C. William Smith

At 12:30 AM, Police Constable William Smith saw Stride talking to a man outside Dutfield's Yard. He described the man as being about 28 years old, 5'7", with a respectable appearance, wearing a dark felt deerstalker hat and dark clothes, and carrying a small newspaper parcel. This man was later seen as one of the stronger suspects, as the timing aligns with when Stride was likely murdered.

Israel Schwartz

At 12:45 AM, Israel Schwartz, a Hungarian immigrant, witnessed what appeared to be an attack on Stride just outside Dutfield's Yard. Schwartz described seeing a man throw Stride to the ground. This man was about 5'5", with a fair complexion, brown hair, and a small brown moustache. He was wearing a dark jacket, dark trousers, and a black cap with a peak. Schwartz also saw a second man, who was 5'11" with light brown hair and a fresh complexion, standing nearby and smoking a pipe. Schwartz was unsure whether this second man was involved, but he hurried away when the first man began shouting at him.

Discovery of the Body

At approximately 1:00 AM, Louis Diemschutz, a market trader returning to Dutfield's Yard with his pony and cart, discovered Stride's body. As he entered the yard, his pony shied away from something lying on the ground. Diemschutz climbed down and found Stride lying on her side, with her face turned toward the wall. He believed she was drunk at first, but when he lifted her head, he realized her throat had been slashed.

Stride was found with her throat cut, the left carotid artery severed in one clean incision. However, unlike the other Ripper victims, there Ire no signs of abdominal mutilation. This has led to the widespread belief that the killer was interrupted, possibly by Diemschutz himself, before he could carry out his usual pattern of violence.

Condition of the Body and Coroner's Report

Dr. Frederick Blackwell's Initial Findings

Dr. Frederick Blackwell, the first medical professional to arrive at the scene, examined Stride's body and provided the following report: "The deceased was lying on her left side, with the face turned towards the wall. Her throat was deeply cut, but there Ire no other visible injuries at first glance. The wound to the throat was approximately 6 inches in length and was made by a sharp instrument, severing the carotid artery and jugular vein."

Dr. George Bagster Phillips' Post-Mortem

Stride's body was later moved to the mortuary, where Dr. George Bagster Phillips conducted a more thorough post-mortem examination. His findings confirmed that the wound to her throat had been inflicted with a single, swift cut. Phillips noted that there was a small amount of blood at the scene, which led him to believe that the killer did not have time to finish his usual method of mutilation.

Phillips stated: "The depth of the incision suggests that the killer acted with great speed and force. It was likely that the blow to the throat killed her almost instantly. There Ire no signs of a struggle, and it appears the killer was in the process of further mutilation when he was interrupted."

Theories of an Interrupted Attack

The lack of mutilation in Stride's case has led most experts to believe that Jack the Ripper was interrupted before he could complete his attack. Many theorists believe that Louis Diemschutz's arrival with his pony and cart scared off the killer, who fled before he could carry out the abdominal mutilations seen in the other cases.

The presence of Israel Schwartz at the scene minutes earlier, along with his description of the second man smoking a pipe, adds another layer of complexity. Some researchers believe that Schwartz may have witnessed an unrelated altercation between Stride and a client or drunken stranger, while others theorize that the man he saw was indeed Jack the Ripper, fleeing the scene as Diemschutz approached.

General Comments

Elizabeth Stride's murder stands out in the Jack the Ripper case because of the apparent interruption that prevented the killer from completing his usual pattern of violence. The multiple eyewitness accounts paint a confusing picture, with descriptions of various men seen with Stride in the hours before her death. The varying descriptions of the killer—English, foreign-looking, stout, thin—have made it difficult to pinpoint the identity of the man who murdered her.

Though the absence of mutilation sets Stride apart from the other victims, the ferocity of the throat wound, the circumstances of her death, and the fact that Catherine Eddowes was killed shortly afterward strongly suggest that Stride was indeed a victim of Jack the Ripper. Her murder, though incomplete by the Ripper's standards, remains a haunting reminder of the violence that gripped the streets of Whitechapel during the Autumn of Terror.

Catherine Eddowes – September 30, 1888

Introduction

The murder of Catherine Eddowes is unique in that it occurred on the same night as the killing of Elizabeth Stride, making September 30, 1888, the infamous "Double Event." Eddowes, a 46-year-old woman with a history of heavy drinking, was found mutilated in Mitre Square, a dark and isolated corner of London, just an hour after Stride was killed. Her death represented a dramatic escalation in the brutality and precision of the Ripper's killings, as evidenced by the extensive mutilation of her face and abdomen.

Timeline of Events and Eyewitness Accounts

Eddowes had been arrested earlier that evening for public drunkenness, and after sobering up, she was released from Bishopsgate Police Station shortly before her death. Several key eyewitnesses provided crucial testimony regarding her final movements and her possible interactions with the killer.

Joseph Lawende

At 1:30 AM, Joseph Lawende, along with two companions, passed by the entrance to Mitre Square. He saw a man and a woman standing and talking near Church Passage. Lawende was able to provide a detailed description of the man, noting that he was about 5'7", with a fair complexion, a brown moustache, and was wearing a pepper-and-salt coat and a red neckerchief. Lawende later identified the woman as Catherine Eddowes, based on the clothing she was wearing when her body was found.

However, Lawende admitted that he did not see the man's face clearly. He described the man's appearance as "sailor-like," and while this description fits a number of men seen around the Ripper murders, it remains speculative.

James Blenkinsop

Also at 1:30 AM, another witness, James Blenkinsop, saw a Ill-dressed man in the vicinity of Mitre Square. While he could not be certain of the man's identity, Blenkinsop's description suggested that Eddowes might have been in the company of a man who was more respectable than many of the other figures involved in the Whitechapel murders.

P.C. Edward Watkins

At 1:44 AM, P.C. Edward Watkins discovered Eddowes' body in Mitre Square while on his regular patrol. Watkins had passed through the square just 15 minutes earlier, indicating that the murder was committed swiftly and with precision. The body was found in a horrific state, with extensive mutilation to her face and abdomen.

Discovery of the Body

When P.C. Watkins discovered Catherine Eddowes' body, she was lying on her back with her clothing pulled up over her abdomen. Her face and body had been viciously mutilated, and it was clear that the killer had been undisturbed while performing the grotesque act. The scene was one of absolute horror.

The key injuries included: - Her throat had been slashed in two deep cuts. - Her face had been extensively mutilated, with the tip of her nose and part of her ear cut off. Deep cuts had been made around her eyes and cheeks. - Her abdomen had been ripped open, and her intestines Ire pulled out and placed over her shoulder, similar to the treatment of Annie Chapman. Part of her left kidney and uterus had been removed.

Condition of the Body and Coroner's Report

Dr. Frederick Gordon Brown's Examination

The post-mortem examination was conducted by Dr. Frederick Gordon Brown, the City of London police surgeon. His report highlighted the disturbing level of skill and speed the killer employed in mutilating Eddowes' body.

Brown stated: "The throat had been cut from ear to ear with deep incisions, and the abdomen was opened by a long, jagged cut. The intestines Ire drawn out of the body and laid over the right shoulder. A piece of flesh, 2 inches by 1 inch, was found detached on the clothing. The left kidney was carefully removed, and a portion of the uterus was missing."

The facial mutilations in Eddowes' case Ire particularly horrifying. Brown described the injuries in detail: "The nose was completely severed, the face was slashed, and both eyelids Ire cut. The right ear was cut through, and there Ire several deep incisions around the eyes and cheeks."

Dr. Brown noted that the killer shold anatomical knowledge, particularly in the removal of the kidney, leading him to speculate that the murderer had some medical or surgical experience.

Escalation in Mutilation

Eddowes' mutilation was significantly more severe than that of the earlier victims, and this escalation in violence has led to various interpretations of the Ripper's psychological state at the time. The facial mutilations were seen as particularly significant, as they appeared to indicate a desire to dehumanize the victim further. The removal of organs with such precision suggested a methodical and calculating approach, unlike the disorganized or frenzied mutilations seen in some of the earlier cases.

Theories and Interpretations of the Eyewitness Testimony

Joseph Lawende's testimony has been one of the most discussed in the case of Catherine Eddowes. His description of a sailor-like man with a brown moustache and pepper-and-salt coat has led some researchers to identify Aaron Kosminski or George Chapman as potential suspects. However, because Lawende did not see the man's face clearly, his testimony remains a point of debate.

Additionally, the sailor-like description matches that of several other men seen around the Whitechapel area at the time, making it difficult to draw definitive conclusions.

The fact that P.C. Watkins had passed through Mitre Square just 15 minutes before discovering the body suggests that the killer worked incredibly quickly. This reinforces the idea that the Ripper was becoming more confident and efficient, capable of carrying out brutal mutilations in a very short period of time without being caught.

The Goulston Street Graffito

One of the most intriguing aspects of the Eddowes case is the Goulston Street graffito, discovered after her murder. A bloody piece of Eddowes' apron was found in Goulston Street, several blocks from Mitre Square, where her body was discovered. Above the apron, written on the wall, was a message that read:

"The Juwes are the men that will not be blamed for nothing".

The exact meaning of this cryptic message has been debated for over a century. Some believe it was a deliberate attempt by the Ripper to frame the local Jewish population, while others think it was unrelated to the crime. The police were divided over whether to erase the message or leave it as evidence. Sir Charles Warren, the Commissioner of Police, famously ordered the writing to be washed off the wall, fearing it would incite anti-Semitic riots in the already tense area of Whitechapel.

General Comments

Catherine Eddowes' murder marked one of the most brutal and meticulously carried out of all the Ripper killings. The combination of the extensive mutilations, the quick and efficient manner of the attack, and the possible eyewitness sightings of the killer all contribute to making this one of the most significant cases in the Jack the Ripper canon. Eddowes' death, along with that of Elizabeth Stride just an hour earlier, underscored the horror and fear that gripped Whitechapel during the Autumn of Terror.

The increasing violence and calculated mutilation of Eddowes' body suggest that the Ripper was becoming more confident in his ability to evade capture. Despite the numerous witnesses who saw a man with Eddowes shortly before her death, no one was ever identified as the killer. The case of Catherine Eddowes remains one of the most chilling in the Ripper saga, and her brutal death continues to haunt researchers and historians to this day.

Mary Jane Kelly – November 9, 1888

Introduction

The murder of Mary Jane Kelly is the most shocking and brutal of all the Jack the Ripper killings. Unlike the other victims, Kelly was murdered indoors, in her small room at 13 Miller's Court, off Dorset Street. This allowed the killer the privacy and time to commit the most extensive mutilations seen in the Ripper series. Kelly's death, on November 9, 1888, marked the final canonical Ripper murder, and her mutilation was so horrific that it shocked even the most experienced investigators.

Timeline of Events and Eyewitness Accounts

Mary Jane Kelly was last seen alive in the early hours of the morning on November 9. Several witnesses reported seeing or hearing Kelly with a man in the hours leading up to her death, though the exact identity of the killer remains unknown. The brutality of the murder, coupled with the fact that it took place in her room, has led to speculation about whether this was the work of Jack the Ripper or a more personal crime. However, the extensive mutilations strongly suggest the same perpetrator.

Mary Ann Cox

At around 11:45 PM on November 8, Mary Ann Cox, a neighbor, saw Kelly in the company of a short, stout man with a blotchy face, wearing a billycock hat and carrying a quart can of beer. Cox, who lived in the same building, reported that Kelly and the man entered her room at 13 Miller's Court together, with Kelly singing, "A violet I plucked from mother's grave when a boy."

Cox heard Kelly singing sporadically until around 1:00 AM, after which the room became silent. She later said she saw no other movements or heard any sounds coming from Kelly's room after that.

George Hutchinson

At around 2:00 AM, George Hutchinson, a man who knew Kelly, claimed to have seen her in the company of a Ill-dressed man. According to Hutchinson's testimony, the man was about 5'6", with dark hair, a pale complexion, and a moustache curled at the ends. He was wearing a long dark coat with astrakhan cuffs and collar, and a red kerchief, and he had a thick gold chain. Hutchinson reported that the man placed his hand on Kelly's shoulder and said something to her in a low voice before they walked together to Miller's Court.

Hutchinson followed the pair but did not intervene, and he later provided a detailed description to the police. His testimony, However, has been treated with skepticism by some researchers, as he waited three days before coming forward and was seen loitering around the crime scene.

Julia Venturney

At 2:30 AM, Julia Venturney, another neighbor, reported hearing a faint cry of "Oh murder!" from Kelly's room. However, this was not an uncommon sound in the slums of Whitechapel, and no one investigated. This cry is believed to be the moment of her murder, though the exact time remains uncertain.

Discovery of the Body

Mary Jane Kelly's body was discovered at 10:45 AM on the morning of November 9 by Thomas Bowyer, the rent collector sent by Kelly's landlord, John McCarthy, to collect overdue rent. Bowyer knocked on Kelly's door but received no response. Upon peering through a broken window, he saw Kelly's mutilated body lying on the bed. Horrified by what he saw, Bowyer rushed to notify McCarthy, who immediately informed the police.

When the police arrived and forced open the door, they Ire met with a scene of unimaginable horror. Kelly's body had been mutilated beyond recognition. The level of violence in her killing far surpassed that of the previous victims, as the killer had ample time and privacy to carry out his gruesome work.

Condition of the Body and Coroner's Report

Dr. Thomas Bond's Report

The post-mortem examination of Mary Jane Kelly was conducted by Dr. Thomas Bond, who provided the following detailed account of her injuries:

"Mary Jane Kelly's body lay on the bed, her head turned to the left side. Her throat had been severed down to the spine, and her entire abdomen and chest had been emptied of organs. The breasts had been cut off, and her face was mutilated beyond recognition. The nose, cheeks, eyebrows, and ears had been partly removed, and there Ire deep gashes in the throat and abdomen. Her uterus, kidneys, and one of her breasts Ire found under her head. Her liver was placed between her feet, and the intestines had been draped over a picture frame."

Bond noted that the extensive mutilation of Kelly's body appeared almost ritualistic in nature, with organs being placed in various parts of the room. The heart was missing and was never recovered.

Dr. George Bagster Phillips' Report

Dr. George Bagster Phillips, who had conducted the post-mortems on previous Ripper victims, also examined Kelly's body. He agreed with Dr. Bond's assessment and added that the killer had displayed considerable anatomical knowledge, particularly in the removal of Kelly's organs.

Phillips stated: "The level of mutilation indicates that the murderer had time and privacy, allowing for a more thorough dissection of the body. The organs Ire removed with precision, similar to what I have seen in previous Ripper cases, but here the mutilation was more extensive and carried out in a more deliberate manner."

Theories and Interpretations of Eyewitness Testimony

George Hutchinson's testimony has sparked considerable debate among Ripperologists. While his detailed description of a Ill-dressed man has been used to support various theories about the killer's identity, some have questioned the credibility of his statement, given the delay in coming forward. Hutchinson described the man as foreign-looking, which led some researchers to focus on suspects like Aaron Kosminski or George Chapman, while others believe Hutchinson himself may have been the killer.

Mary Ann Cox's account of the blotchy-faced man seen with Kelly earlier in the evening has also raised questions. This man, described as short and stout, did not match Hutchinson's description of the Ill-dressed man, leading some to believe that Kelly may have entertained more than one visitor that night, or that one of the descriptions was inaccurate.

General Comments

The murder of Mary Jane Kelly marked the culmination of Jack the Ripper's killing spree, and it remains one of the most brutal and disturbing acts of violence in criminal history. Unlike the previous victims, Kelly's murder occurred indoors, giving the killer time and privacy to indulge in his most horrific fantasies. The level of mutilation inflicted on Kelly's body was unprecedented, even by the Ripper's standards, and it is believed that her death marked the end of his reign of terror.

Despite the extensive evidence surrounding Kelly's murder—including eyewitness testimonies, detailed post-mortem reports, and the fact that the crime scene was left largely undisturbed—the identity of her killer remains a mystery. The varying accounts of the men seen with Kelly in the hours leading up to her death have only added to the confusion, and the Ripper's true identity continues to elude even the most dedicated investigators.

Mary Jane Kelly's death represents the darkest chapter in the Autumn of Terror, and her murder stands as a chilling reminder of the brutal and inexplicable nature of the crimes committed by Jack the Ripper.

Chapter 3

Literature in Ripperology

Well, where do I begin, and how? Do I piss on people? I suppose the adult thing to do here is to comment on whatever aspects of literature I find useful, and save pissing for when I cannot help myself.

I suppose Stephen Knight's book bears mentioning. According to him, his royal highness Prince Albert Victor, Queen Victoria's grandson, had impregnated one of the five canonical victims. I forget which. Apparently the kid was born, and had a rightful claim to the throne, which people didn't like for some reason. Also apparently one of them gave his highness syphilis or something. So Queen Victoria, who was rather miffed with the whole affair, decided that it would please her majesty to rid her realm of these five prostitutes. Oh, and one more thing, apparently the one who had Victor's child told the other four, as one does. And Queen Victoria found out about it, as one does. The prostitutes thought it would be a good idea to blackmail the royal family apparently, choosing to disregard the obvious power imbalance here. As one does. So her royal highness charged her close personal loony doctor, Sir William Gull, loony doctor extraordinary, ABC, DEF, FCCB, FSHIT, FRSCl, and various other F's, to go finish off the five friends.

My problem with this, notwithstanding the fact that the loony doc extraordinary had had a stroke, couldn't get out of bed, and the idea of a grandpa brandishing his surgeons knife, shuffling around Whitechapel chatting up seductive ladies of the night somehow doesn't compute in my simple brain, much like my problem with Bruce Robinson's theory which I'll discuss in the next paragraph, is that conspiracy theories are too complicated and are almost never true. They assume that the conspiracy dudes are competent, and that they can keep a secret. They are usually neither. And old pop Sir William Gull wasn't as young and resilient as he was in his loony doctor training days.

Some claim that his royal highness himself was instructed in the intricate art of sword brandishing by his mentor, pop William. And HRH did the dispatching himself, because he was taking revenge for the syphilis. But the dude wasn't in London at the time of the murders. This what I mean by story and counter story. It's all a maze made of bullshit.

Oh, but Bruce Robinson. They all love Jack. Busting the Ripper. I've got no animosity for Bruce Robinson—far from it, in fact. The man has done his research, and nobody can deny the depth of his investigation. He's dug into archives, sifted through countless records, and brought a level of detail that few others have matched. And let's be honest, Michael Maybrick was a bad dude. There's no doubt about that. But he just wasn't Jack the Ripper.

Now, Bruce Robinson's argument, while imaginative and Ill-researched, relies on a

CHAPTER 3. LITERATURE IN RIPPEROLOGY

few shaky assumptions. Let's walk through the key points of his theory and examine where it starts to unravel.

1. Everybody was a Mason Robinson's theory rests heavily on the idea that Freemasons Ire at the heart of the Ripper murders. In his view, it wasn't just that Michael Maybrick was a Freemason, but that nearly everyone involved—police officers, doctors, officials—was also part of the brotherhood. This, according to Robinson, explains the elaborate cover-up that allegedly took place. But here's the problem: even if many of the men involved Ire Freemasons, there's no evidence that this had anything to do with the murders. The idea of an entire secret society orchestrating a cover-up for one man stretches credulity. Cover-ups on that scale rarely succeed for long, let alone for over a century. The more people involved, the harder it is to keep a secret, and in this case, no hard evidence has ever emerged to support such a grand conspiracy. It's not enough to say, "they Ire all Masons," and leave it at that.

2. The Masons were covering up for the killer Even if I entertain the idea that many individuals involved Ire Masons, there's no direct proof that they Ire actively shielding the Ripper. Robinson's theory presupposes that the Freemasons Ire not only aware of Maybrick's crimes but that they Ire willing to let the brutal murders of innocent women go unpunished to protect one of their own. This leap is where things really start to fall apart. The idea that a secret society, full of men of varying social ranks and responsibilities, would prioritize protecting a serial killer over their own reputations and lives is, at best, far-fetched. To believe this, I would need actual evidence of Masonic involvement in the investigations, and Robinson simply doesn't provide that. His argument relies more on insinuation than hard proof.

3. The Maybrick Diary is genuine The Maybrick Diary—allegedly written by James Maybrick, Michael's brother—has been a major piece of Robinson's puzzle. In his theory, the diary is used to frame James Maybrick for the Ripper murders, with Michael as the actual culprit. However, the diary has been discredited time and again. It is widely considered a forgery by experts, and even the people who discovered it have raised doubts about its authenticity. If the diary is fake, then much of Robinson's theory falls apart. You can't build a solid case on a foundation that is so demonstrably flaId. Without the diary's credibility, the connection between Michael Maybrick and the murders becomes far more tenuous.

4. Maybrick killed the prostitutes to fulfill a twisted fantasy of killing his brother's wife over and over again This part of Robinson's theory gets into deeply speculative territory. According to him, Michael Maybrick harbored a pathological hatred for his brother's wife, Florence Maybrick, and sought to relive the fantasy of killing her by murdering the Whitechapel prostitutes. Not only is this an extraordinary claim, but it's also one that lacks supporting evidence. There's no clear indication that Michael had this kind of psychological fixation or that the murders Ire in any way related to his brother's marital problems. In fact, the connection between the Ripper killings and any personal vendetta Michael might have had is incredibly Iak. It requires us to accept that a highly successful and public figure would risk everything to play out a private revenge fantasy—one that nobody else seemed to know about.

5. Maybrick wrote the diary and framed his brother This final point is perhaps the most convoluted. Robinson argues that Michael Maybrick not only committed the murders but also wrote the Maybrick Diary in order to frame his brother, James. But again, this assumes that the diary is genuine, which, as I've already covered, it is not. Furthermore, this theory suggests that Michael was both devious enough to carry out the

CHAPTER 3. LITERATURE IN RIPPEROLOGY

murders and sophisticated enough to fabricate a detailed written confession implicating his brother. This is a convoluted motive that, without strong supporting evidence, feels more like a stretch than a legitimate explanation.

But let's be clear: Robinson's work is valuable. He brought fresh attention to the case, sparked discussions, and helped illuminate parts of the history that might otherwise have been left in the shadows. I just happen to part ways on the conclusions. Michael Maybrick? Sure, a villain. Jack the Ripper? No, not quite.

But Robinson does highlight an avenue of research in Ripperology that is often ignored or discounted: the alleged Ripper correspondence, and the matter of Matthew Packer, the grape seller who claimed to have seen Elizabeth Stride before her murder. Most researchers agree that the bulk of Ripper letters—at least those known to us—were likely hoaxes or press-driven profiteering. Yet two letters in particular stand out for me, and examining them alongside the well-known *"Dear Boss"* and *"Saucy Jacky"* missives offers some thought-provoking insights.

Let us consider the three communications in question:

- **The Dear Boss Letter (September 25, 1888):** Cocky, mocking, and relatively polished in grammar and spelling. Here, the writer first adopts the moniker "Jack the Ripper" and speaks of "funny little games" and the intention to clip a victim's ears to send to the police.

- **The Saucy Jacky Postcard (October 1, 1888):** Shorter and slightly less polished, but still taunting and boastful. It refers to the recent "double event" (the murders of Elizabeth Stride and Catherine Eddowes) as though fulfilling a promise made in the earlier letter. The tone remains one of derision and challenge, aimed at the authorities and the public.

- **The Matthew Packer Letter (Date Uncertain):** After Matthew Packer sold grapes to a couple (potentially Stride and her killer) and later spoke to the police, he reportedly received a letter threatening him personally. This letter claims to be from "Jack the Ripper" and shares thematic similarities with the "Dear Boss" communication, particularly references to a "little game" and the mutilation of ears. Here is the full text as it is commonly cited:

    > *You though your-self very clever I reckon when you informed the police. But you made a mistake if you though I dident see you. Now I known you know me and I see your little game, and I mean to finish you and send your ears to your wife if you show this to the police or help them if you do I will finish you. It no use your trying to get out of my way. Because I have you when you dont expect it and I keep my word as you soon see and rip you up. Yours truly Jack the Ripper. PS You see I know your address*

Comparing these three communications, we note several common threads. First, both the Dear Boss letter and the Packer letter speak of "little games" and the intention to cut off ears, strongly suggesting a link in mindset or authorship. The Dear Boss letter promised to clip ears and send them to the police, while the Packer letter threatens to send Packer's ears to his wife. The recurring fixation on ears as tokens of mutilation and intimidation is telling, as is the consistent use of the "Jack the Ripper" signature.

Meanwhile, the Saucy Jacky postcard, though not mentioning ears or "little games" explicitly, reinforces the persona established in Dear Boss and seems to confirm the promise of further violence. The thematic chain running from Dear Boss to Saucy Jacky and then to the Packer letter suggests a continuum of threats and psychological play. The first two communications openly mock the authorities and the public, taking a performative delight in their inability to stop the killer. The Packer letter, by contrast, personalizes this threat, implying that the author is willing to silence a witness who dared to inform the police.

One could argue that the Packer letter might be an imitator's work. Its grammar and spelling are less polished, and the tone is more direct and personal. Yet this could be deliberate obfuscation, or simply a sign of writing under different circumstances. Given the consistent themes—games, ear mutilation, and the Ripper's signature—it seems less likely that this is a random hoax by someone with no knowledge of the earlier letters. Instead, it may indicate that Packer truly saw something he should not have, prompting a genuine threat from the same mind that produced the earlier taunts.

If that is the case, then Robinson's attention to the Packer letter is indeed valuable. It draws focus to a detail frequently omitted or underemphasized in other Ripper studies, providing a potentially illuminating clue about the genuine killer's mindset and motivations. One need not fully accept the premise to appreciate the significance of the evidence. At the very least, it sparks worthwhile debate, shining a light on the darker corners of the Whitechapel murders and the tangled web of real and forged communications that surround them.

Before I go any further, let me offer this disclaimer: When I reference or quote other authors or sources in this book, there is always the possibility that I may be misquoting or inaccurately paraphrasing their work. The details I ascribe to them may not be entirely correct, and I encourage readers to independently verify any claims or statements I attribute to other writers. Nothing I present here should be taken as a definitive representation of their ideas or as a basis for any legal or defamatory actions. This book is meant for exploration and analysis, and any errors in representation are entirely unintentional.

Speaking of stories often overlooked in mainstream Ripperology, there's also the matter of Fiona Kendall Lane and her family's claim to possess insider knowledge about Jack the Ripper's identity. According to her, John McCarthy, the landlord of Mary Jane Kelly, was her great-grandfather, and he supposedly knew the identity of the Ripper. The family legend, passed down through generations, is that McCarthy saw the man who entered Mary Kelly's room on that fateful night. And if the tale is to be believed, this man was Samuel Barnett, a clergyman and social reformer in Whitechapel.

Now, let's take a moment to appreciate the sheer abundance of stories like this in the Ripper case. For every suspect, there's a new claim, a family story, or a supposed eyewitness who was never documented at the time. In Kendall Lane's version, Barnett is the Ripper—a theory that raises more questions than answers. For one, Barnett, as a man of the cloth, doesn't quite fit the psychological profile of a sadistic serial killer. And while there's a certain appeal to the idea of a respected figure hiding in plain sight, it feels more like another layer of myth added to the fog surrounding the case.

To her credit, Kendall Lane tried to bring her family's story to light, posting about it on Ripper forums and sharing her side of the legend. Unfortunately, she was largely met with skepticism and even ridicule. But here's the thing: stories like these are a dime a dozen in Ripperology. For every tale, there's a counter-tale. For every supposed witness,

CHAPTER 3. LITERATURE IN RIPPEROLOGY

there's another witness claiming something entirely different. It's the very nature of this case, a swirling vortex of anecdotes, memories, and myths that often lead nowhere.

Yet, I'll say this—these personal stories, whether credible or not, add a human dimension to a case that has become larger than life. They remind us that, at its core, the Jack the Ripper mystery is a story of real people, real lives, and real horrors. And if nothing else, Fiona Kendall Lane gave us one more story to ponder in this endless maze of speculation.

It's important to note that the suspect Barnett I've mentioned here is listed by Trevor Marriott as Fiona Kendall Lane's suspect, and I'm basing this on my recollection from a one-year-old reading of Marriott's book. As with all quotes and references, I encourage readers to verify this independently. Furthermore, the account of Kendall Lane being ridiculed on Ripper forums is hearsay, and I cannot personally verify the details. This is simply part of the broader narrative surrounding the case, and as with much of Ripperology, it should be taken with a healthy dose of skepticism.

Let's cover a bit more stuff before moving on.

Aaron Kosminski frequently appears in Jack the Ripper literature as a prominent suspect, his name surfacing in both police reports and subsequent investigations. His candidacy gained particular traction after a controversial 2014 DNA analysis, which purportedly linked his genetic material to a shawl allegedly found at the scene of Catherine Eddowes' murder. Coupled with Kosminski's poorly documented mental illness and his residence in the Whitechapel area, these claims led some to consider him a prime suspect in the Ripper killings.

Influential figures in the original investigation seem to have leaned toward Kosminski as well. Sir Robert Anderson and Chief Inspector Donald Swanson each implied that Kosminski was the most likely culprit. In the so-called "Swanson Marginalia," an annotation Swanson made in his own copy of Anderson's memoirs, he noted that a suspect—widely believed to be Kosminski—had been identified by a witness. According to Swanson, this witness recognized the suspect but refused to testify, effectively halting any legal action. This narrative has fueled speculation that the police "knew" the Ripper's identity but were stymied by procedural and evidentiary limitations.

Additional intrigue arises from how Anderson may have interpreted the infamous Goulston Street Graffito. Discovered near a bloody piece of Eddowes' apron, the message read: "The Juwes are the men that will not be blamed for nothing." Anderson, already suspicious of local Jewish immigrants, allegedly saw this message as indicative of a Polish-Jewish culprit. In some tellings, he believed the phrase made more sense in Polish, a language known for double negatives. Though the validity of this linguistic interpretation is highly questionable, it appears that Anderson became fixated on the idea of a Polish Jew as the killer—a fixation that centered on Kosminski once the suspect was eventually confined to an asylum.

However, several critical points undermine this theory. Foremost is the much-publicized DNA analysis, which has been roundly criticized. Detractors argue that the shawl in question has an uncertain provenance; it may not have come from the crime scene at all. Its chain of custody is unclear, and the tests lacked the methodological rigor required to conclusively link Kosminski's DNA to the murders.

Additionally, questions remain about Kosminski's mental state and capabilities. He suffered from severe schizophrenia and was later admitted to a lunatic asylum. While his institutionalization might explain why the murders ceased, it is difficult to reconcile such an erratic, severely impaired individual with the meticulous dissection and anatomical knowledge often ascribed to the Ripper. The notion of a cunning killer who evaded capture through careful planning and skill does not sit comfortably alongside a man struggling with severe mental health issues.

One crucial element of the case against Kosminski involves the identity of "Swanson's witness." Many researchers believe the witness in question was Israel Schwartz, who reportedly saw a man assaulting Elizabeth Stride on the night of her murder. According to some interpretations, Schwartz was later confronted with the suspect—allegedly Kosminski—and immediately identified him as the man he had seen. Yet even here, the narrative frays. For one, Kosminski was not committed to an asylum until 1891, well after the main body of the murders. Moreover, he did not die shortly thereafter, but lived under care until 1919. If Schwartz's identification indeed took place, it is also a significant leap to go from witnessing Kosminski shoving Stride to labeling him the Ripper responsible for all the canonical murders. Notably, Elizabeth Stride's status as a Ripper victim remains hotly debated, and some experts do not consider her murder part of the canonical sequence. Thus, building an entire theory around this single, disputed identification stretches credulity.

In light of these problems, the so-called "Kosminski Theory" appears increasingly fragile. Without robust physical evidence, and with the lingering concerns about witness reliability and the difficulties in matching Kosminski's profile to that of a brutal, anatomically skilled killer, the case seems more like an artifact of Victorian-era prejudice and police uncertainty than a definitive solution to the mystery.

In the end, the enduring popularity of Kosminski as a suspect may reflect the allure of having a suspect singled out by key investigators, rather than any decisive proof. It suggests a scenario in which the police, lacking concrete evidence and desperate for a resolution, latched onto the figure of a disturbed man living in their midst. The entire narrative may well have been an amateur attempt to salvage official credibility—an effort by officers who were uncertain, overwhelmed, and struggling to save face. As a result, what we see in the Kosminski Theory may be less the genuine unmasking of a monstrous criminal and more the scapegoating of a vulnerable individual who simply fit into a preconceived narrative.

James Maybrick, a Liverpool cotton merchant, entered the Ripper suspect pool in a dramatic way—with the discovery of the Maybrick Diary. This diary, which surfaced in the 1990s, purportedly details Maybrick's confessions to the Ripper murders. Written in a chilling, almost gleeful tone, the diary recounts the killings and expresses Maybrick's satisfaction in outwitting the police. The diary's authenticity, However, has been the subject of intense debate, with many experts calling it an outright forgery.

The Maybrick Diary describes Maybrick's troubled marriage to his wife, Florence, and his gradual descent into murderous madness. The diary paints a picture of a man consumed with hatred for his wife and, by extension, the women he murdered in Whitechapel. According to the text, Maybrick killed the prostitutes as part of a twisted revenge fantasy, imagining that each one was his wife, allowing him to act out his desire to kill her over and over again.

While the diary provides tantalizing details, including supposed insights into the Ripper's psyche, its origins are highly suspicious. From the beginning, critics have pointed out several inconsistencies in the text. For one, there are discrepancies between the language used in the diary and that of the late 19th century. Further, forensic analysis of the ink and paper has suggested that the diary was created much more recently than 1888, leading many to conclude that it is a modern forgery.

Yet, despite these issues, the Maybrick Diary has attracted a following. Supporters argue that the diary offers an unprecedented glimpse into the mind of the Ripper, and that it contains details only the killer would know. The fact that Maybrick's own life was marked by turmoil—he was poisoned, possibly by his wife, and died in 1889—adds to the intrigue.

If the diary were genuine, it would be a bombshell in Ripperology, offering what seems to be a full confession. But the consensus among historians and Ripperologists is that it is a hoax. Still, the theory around James Maybrick persists, not least because it fits into the broader narrative of an upper-class killer hiding in plain sight. Whether through the diary or otherwise, the Maybrick name continues to hold a place in the Ripper suspect pool, though it rests on quicksand. Personally, I think it's a bucket of horse refuse.

Montague John Druitt is often mentioned in the early years of Ripperology, primarily due to the Macnaghten Memorandum, which named him as one of the top suspects. Druitt was a barrister and schoolteacher, Ill-educated and from a respectable background, but his personal life was troubled. He was dismissed from his teaching job in late 1888, and shortly afterward, he committed suicide by drowning in the Thames. His body was found in early December 1888, just weeks after the last of the canonical Ripper murders.

For many, this timeline appeared to fit—Druitt's death roughly coincided with the end of the Whitechapel murders, leading some to speculate that he ended his own life out of guilt. Sir Melville Macnaghten, in his famous memorandum, stated that Druitt was "sexually insane," which has been interpreted by some to mean he had a violent, suppressed nature that might have erupted in the form of the Ripper murders.

However, there are several glaring problems with the Druitt theory. Perhaps the most damning is that the day before one of the murders, Druitt was playing cricket far from London. He was listed on a cricket match score sheet, placing him in Dorset during the time one of the murders was being committed. For Druitt to have taken part in the murder, he would have needed to swiftly catch a train back to Whitechapel, don his serial killer costume, and then perform the brutal, calculated mutilations associated with the Ripper—all without anyone noticing. The logistics alone make this scenario improbable, if not downright impossible.

While Druitt's personal troubles and eventual suicide may raise eyebrows, the practicalities of placing him at the scene of the murders simply don't add up. His alibi, combined with the lack of any solid evidence linking him to the crimes, effectively eliminates him as a practical suspect. Another one bites the dust.

David Cohen, a Polish Jew with violent tendencies, has gained attention primarily through the work of Martin Fido, who proposed that Cohen may have been the actual identity of Jack the Ripper. In this theory, Nathan Kaminsky—another Polish Jew who was once suspected—was an alias used by Cohen. Fido's theory rests on the idea that Cohen was a violent, deranged man who was committed to an asylum right around the time the Ripper murders ceased. This, combined with his proximity to Whitechapel and his erratic behavior, makes him a plausible suspect in Fido's eyes.

Cohen was known for his extreme violence, and his incarceration after the final Ripper killing provides a timeline that, at first glance, makes sense. The theory argues that Aaron Kosminski, long suspected by some police officials, was a misidentification of Cohen/Kaminsky—as both were Polish Jews with mental illnesses who lived in Whitechapel. Sir Robert Anderson and Donald Swanson's convictions about a Polish Jew being the culprit further lend some weight to the idea, but this is where the theory starts to blur.

However, there is a significant problem: David Cohen was far less organized and methodical than the man described in the Jack the Ripper murders. While Cohen's history of violence could fit the profile of a murderer, the Ripper shold a certain anatomical knowledge, as well as a chilling ability to evade capture—traits that seem far beyond Cohen's apparent capabilities. Moreover, Cohen's madness was unrelenting, making it difficult to reconcile his profile with the brutal but seemingly controlled acts of the Ripper.

While the Cohen/Kaminsky theory presents a tidy solution to the question of Jack the Ripper, the suspect's psychological state seems too chaotic for the calculated and ritualistic nature of the Ripper's crimes. In the end, Cohen's violence and confinement at the time the murders ended make him a compelling figure, but his inability to match the more refined aspects of the Ripper leaves lingering doubt. Like many suspects, Cohen fits the timeline, but his behavior doesn't fully align with what I know about the killer.

One of the more intriguing suspects in recent years is **Charles Cross**, or as he is now known, Charles Lechmere. Lechmere was the man who "discovered" the body of Mary Ann Nichols in Buck's Row on the morning of her murder. For years, Cross was simply regarded as a witness—a passerby who stumbled upon the body on his way to work. But more recent scrutiny has raised the possibility that Lechmere may, in fact, have been the killer.

Lechmere's movements that night are suspicious. He claimed to have been on his way to work, yet when he found Nichols' body, he did not immediately raise the alarm. Instead, he waited for another passerby, Robert Paul, and together they inspected the body before heading off to find a constable. Lechmere gave his name as Charles Cross to the police, using the name of his stepfather, a detail that some believe indicates a desire to avoid detection.

More tellingly, Lechmere's route to work passed near the locations of the other Ripper murders, and his work schedule lines up suspiciously Ill with the times the killings took place. Additionally, the area where he lived—Doveton Street—was in close proximity to all the murder sites. Some researchers, like Christer Holmgren, have suggested that Lechmere might have been disturbed during his killing of Nichols and pretended to be an innocent bystander when Paul approached.

What makes Lechmere such a compelling suspect is that, unlike others, he was actually at the scene of a murder. His proximity to the crime scenes and the ease with which he could have blended into the local environment make him a plausible Ripper candidate. There's also the fact that Lechmere had ample opportunity to commit the murders while appearing to go about his daily life. His unassuming nature and his role as a cartman gave him the freedom to move through the streets of Whitechapel without raising suspicion.

While there's no hard evidence linking Lechmere to the murders, the theory provides a coherent narrative that ties together the geography, timing, and actions of a man long regarded as a mere witness. His role as a discoverer of Nichols' body has transformed him into a serious suspect. Like many others, the case against Charles Lechmere relies on circumstantial evidence, but when combined with his proximity to the crimes, his hidden identity, and his suspicious behavior on the night of Nichols' murder, it's difficult to dismiss him outright.

Chapter 4
My Analysis

Witness	Which Scene?	Time / Appearance
Emily Walter (?)	Annie Chapman	2:00 A.M. Foreigner aged 37, dark beard and moustache. wearing short dark jacket, dark vest and trousers, black scarf, and black felt hat.
Elizabeth Long	Annie Chapman	5:30 A.M. Dark complexion, brown deerstalker hat, possibly a dark overcoat. Aged over 40, somewhat taller than Chapman. A foreigner of "shabby genteel."
J. Best and John Gardner	Elizabeth Stride	11:00 P.M. 5'5" tall, English, black moustache, sandy eyelashes, Iak, wearing a morning suit and a hat.
William Marshall	Elizabeth Stride	11:45 P.M. Small, black coat, dark trousers, middle-aged, round cap with a small sailor-like peak. 5'6", stout, appearance of a clerk. No moustache, no gloves, with a cutaway coat.
Matthew Packer	Elizabeth Stride	12:00 - 12:30 A.M. Aged 25-30, 5'7", long black coat buttoned up, soft felt hat, broad shoulders. Maybe a young clerk, frock coat, no gloves.
P.C. William Smith	Elizabeth Stride	12:30 A.M. Aged 28, clean-shaven and respectable appearance, 5'7", hard dark felt deerstalker hat, dark clothes. Carrying a newspaper parcel 18 x 7 inches.
James Brown	Elizabeth Stride	12:45 A.M. 5'7", stout, long black diagonal coat which reached almost to his heels.
Israel Schwartz	Elizabeth Stride	12:45 A.M. First man: Aged 30, 5'5", brown haired, fair complexion, small brown moustache, full face, broad shoulders, dark jacket and trousers, black cap with peak. Second man: Aged 35, 5'11", fresh complexion, light brown hair, dark overcoat, old black hard felt hat with a wide brim, clay pipe.

CHAPTER 4. MY ANALYSIS

Joseph Lawende	Catherine Eddowes	1:30 A.M. Aged 30, 5'7", fair complexion, brown moustache, salt-and-pepper coat, red neckerchief, grey peaked cloth cap. Sailor-like.
James Blenkinsop	Catherine Eddowes	1:30 A.M. Ill-dressed.
Mary Ann Cox	Mary Kelly	11:45 P.M. Short, stout man, shabbily dressed. Billycock hat, blotchy face, carroty moustache, holding quart can of beer.
George Hutchinson	Mary Kelly	2:00 A.M. Aged 34-35, 5'6", pale complexion, dark hair, slight moustache curled at each end, long dark coat, collar and cuffs of astrakhan, dark jacket underneath. Light waistcoat, thick gold chain with a red stone seal, dark trousers, and button boots, gaiters, white buttons. White shirt, black tie fastened with a horseshoe pin. Dark hat, turned down in middle. Red kerchief. Jewish and respectable in appearance.

The table of eyewitness accounts. These are the sole evidence that I have, collected not from stories of what may have happened at mortuaries, at inquests or within the offices of the metropolitan police, they speak not of territorial snafus, or negligent medical examinations, not of cryptic graffito, of pieces of strewn apron, and as a collection, they are not biased, they cannot be, as they are drawn from different people, taken from an independent and identically distributed sample. Here, dear reader, lies the truth, hidden in these accounts, waiting to be uncovered, is, and indeed, must necessarily be, a photograph of the man behind the knife.

I began this journey with a sense of hope, eager to discover the hidden truth within the eyewitness accounts. As I inspected the initial table, with each witness providing their observations, I was struck by the sheer variety of descriptions. Some witnesses spoke of foreigners with dark complexions and beards, others mentioned Ill-dressed men with a polished appearance, while still others described short, stout, shabby figures, whose features seemed to blend into the fog of Whitechapel.

At first glance, it appeared that the descriptions referred to five or six entirely different men. I found myself in the same predicament that had confounded Ripperologists for years: faced with the apparent reality that these accounts Ire irreconcilable, that they described an assortment of characters, each distinct from the others. How could one man be a foreigner with a dark beard in one instance, and then be clean-shaven and respectable a few hours later? How could the killer be both short and stout, yet tall and broad-shouldered?

This inconsistency led to a growing sense of frustration. I began to understand why so many researchers had disregarded these accounts as unreliable. It seemed impossible for these descriptions to point to a single person. As much as I wanted to believe that the truth was hidden within the testimonies of these witnesses, the overwhelming differences led me to a moment of doubt, where the easiest conclusion was to dismiss them entirely. I shared the common belief that the eyewitness accounts could not possibly converge into one profile.

But then, I began to wonder if there Ire clusters to be found, if one individual could not cover these differences, how many distinct individuals would be needed? Was the Ripper actually two different people, or maybe there Ire three or four, and I made a mistake by assuming that this was the work of one man? Is every description irreconcilable with every other description? Surely not. So I began to search for clusters, baskets into which to put each account.

As I began to sift through the details in these accounts, I naturally attempted to organize them, grouping descriptions into clusters based on what seemed like common features. At this stage, the process felt straightforward—almost clinical. The entries aligned into patterns, each cluster taking shape as if representing a different man, adding to our sense of confusion.

Cluster 1: The "Dark-bearded Foreigners" (Annie Chapman Scene)

- **Emily Walter (Annie Chapman, 2:00 A.M.)**: Foreigner, aged 37, dark beard and moustache, black felt hat, dark jacket, vest, and trousers.
- **Elizabeth Long (Annie Chapman, 5:30 A.M.)**: Dark complexion, brown deerstalker hat, foreigner of "shabby genteel," dark overcoat.

These witnesses described a man with a foreign appearance, dark features, and a tendency toward shabbiness.

Cluster 2: The "Morning Suit Englishman" (Elizabeth Stride Scene)

- **J. Best and John Gardner (Elizabeth Stride, 11:00 P.M.)**: English, black moustache, sandy eyelashes, wearing a morning suit and a hat, 5'5".
- **William Marshall (Elizabeth Stride, 11:45 P.M.)**: Middle-aged, small, black coat, dark trousers, clerk-like appearance, 5'6", stout, no moustache.

These descriptions referred to a small, stout man with English features, but the question of the moustache added confusion.

Cluster 3: The "Respectable Man with Dark Clothing" (Elizabeth Stride Scene)

- **Matthew Packer (Elizabeth Stride, 12:00 A.M.)**: Aged 25-30, long black coat, broad shoulders, frock coat, no gloves, soft felt hat.
- **P.C. William Smith (Elizabeth Stride, 12:30 A.M.)**: Aged 28, clean-shaven, 5'7", respectable appearance, dark clothes, dark deerstalker hat, carrying a newspaper parcel.
- **James Brown (Elizabeth Stride, 12:45 A.M.)**: 5'7", stout, long black coat reaching almost to his heels.

Cluster 4: The "Two Men Involved" (Israel Schwartz Witnessing Two Men)

- **First Man**: Aged 30, 5'5", brown haired, brown moustache, broad shoulders, dark jacket and trousers, black cap.
- **Second Man**: Aged 35, 5'11", fresh complexion, light brown hair, dark overcoat, old black felt hat, clay pipe.

Two distinct men Ire seen by Israel Schwartz, potentially complicating the identification.

Cluster 5: The "Sailor-like Man" (Catherine Eddowes Scene)

- **Joseph Lawende (Catherine Eddowes, 1:30 A.M.)**: Aged 30, 5'7", fair complexion, brown moustache, salt-and-pepper coat, sailor-like grey peaked cap.
- **James Blenkinsop (Catherine Eddowes, 1:30 A.M.)**: Ill-dressed.

These witnesses described a Ill-dressed man with sailor-like features, adding to the confusion of appearances.

Cluster 6: The "Shabby Man with Billycock Hat" (Mary Kelly Scene)

- **Mary Ann Cox (Mary Kelly, 11:45 P.M.)**: Short, stout, shabbily dressed, blotchy face, billycock hat, carroty moustache.

This description pointed to a man with disheveled appearance, but noticeably stout with a distinctive hat.

Cluster 7: The Dandy (Mary Kelly Scene)

- **George Hutchinson (Mary Kelly, 2:00 A.M.)**: Aged 34-35, pale complexion, slight moustache curled at the ends, wearing a long dark coat with astrakhan cuffs and collar, dark trousers, white shirt, gaiters, gold chain, dark felt hat turned down in the middle, Jewish, respectable appearance.

This was a man of elegance, dressed in finer clothing than the others, appearing almost out of place in Whitechapel's dark, dingy streets—a figure that drew suspicion precisely because he seemed too polished for his surroundings.

After struggling with the initial division into several clusters, I noticed that one key element—the *deerstalker* hat—was a striking and distinctive feature. The deerstalker hat was mentioned in multiple eyewitness accounts, and its unique shape made it unlikely to be a coincidence. This realization prompted us to attempt merging all the deerstalker sightings into a single cluster. As I analyzed the descriptions, I also noticed that some witnesses used the term *felt hat*, with one witness explicitly mentioning both "felt" and "deerstalker" simultaneously to describe the hat.

This overlap suggested a second possibility: that the deerstalker and felt hats might be the same or similar in some cases, and therefore, I could consider merging all felt hat sightings with the deerstalker mentions. However, as with any synthesis, I found disagreements within both clusters, which needed to be acknowledged.

Cluster 1: Merging Deerstalker Sightings

I began by merging all descriptions that explicitly mentioned a *deerstalker* hat:

- **Elizabeth Long (Annie Chapman, 5:30 A.M.)**: Described the suspect as having a brown deerstalker hat, dark complexion, possibly a dark overcoat, and shabby genteel appearance.

- **P.C. William Smith (Elizabeth Stride, 12:30 A.M.)**: Reported seeing a man wearing a hard dark felt *deerstalker* hat, clean-shaven, 5'7", respectable appearance, and carrying a newspaper parcel.

- **James Brown (Elizabeth Stride, 12:45 A.M.)**: Described a man with a long black diagonal coat, 5'7", stout, and wearing a *felt hat* (the type of felt hat was not explicitly stated as a deerstalker, but it was dark, and the context suggests a similar look).

Disagreements within this cluster:

- **Facial Hair**: Elizabeth Long's suspect was not explicitly stated as clean-shaven, while P.C. William Smith's suspect was clean-shaven, and the man seen by James Brown was stout but facial hair was not noted.

- **Complexion**: Elizabeth Long described a dark-complexioned man, while P.C. Smith's description focused on a clean-shaven, respectable-looking man, which might imply a lighter complexion, though this is speculative.

- **Occupation Implied by Appearance**: Elizabeth Long mentioned the "shabby genteel" nature of the suspect, suggesting a man of lower economic standing, while P.C. Smith described a "respectable" man, hinting at a difference in social class.

Cluster 2: Merging Deerstalkers and Felt Hat Sightings

Taking it a step further, I considered that the term *felt hat* could overlap with *deerstalker* in many instances. One witness even described the hat as both *felt* and *deerstalker*, suggesting that these might not be entirely different:

- **Elizabeth Long (Annie Chapman, 5:30 A.M.)**: Brown deerstalker hat, dark complexion, foreigner of "shabby genteel."

- **P.C. William Smith (Elizabeth Stride, 12:30 A.M.)**: Hard dark *felt deerstalker* hat, clean-shaven, respectable, and carrying a newspaper parcel.

- **James Brown (Elizabeth Stride, 12:45 A.M.)**: Described the suspect wearing a long black diagonal coat, stout, 5'7", and a *felt hat*.

- **George Hutchinson (Mary Kelly, 2:00 A.M.)**: Slight moustache, curled at the ends, wearing a long dark coat with astrakhan cuffs, gaiters, white shirt, thick gold chain, and a dark *felt hat* turned down in the middle.

- **Matthew Packer (Elizabeth Stride, 12:00 A.M.)**: Described the man as wearing a *soft felt hat* along with a long black coat and broad shoulders.

Disagreements within this broader cluster:

- **Hat Type**: While some witnesses specified *deerstalker*, others used the broader term *felt hat*, which might imply a similar style but could also refer to other types of felt hats.

- **Facial Hair**: The facial hair descriptions varied greatly—some men Ire clean-shaven (P.C. Smith's account), while others had moustaches (Hutchinson and Packer's descriptions), and James Brown did not mention facial hair at all.

- **Class and Respectability**: As with the first cluster, there was a mix of descriptions suggesting different social classes. Hutchinson's "respectable" man dressed in fine astrakhan and gold chains contrasts with Packer's broader-shouldered, perhaps younger clerk-like figure, and James Brown's "stout" figure seemed less refined.

- **Body Type**: James Brown and Matthew Packer described a "stout" man, while P.C. Smith's suspect seemed more average in build, and Hutchinson's figure was not described as stout.

In both clusters, I found disagreements, but merging based on the common element of the *hat* allowed us to reduce the confusion slightly and start seeing potential overlaps. It became clear that while the hats might match, the other features—such as facial hair, body type, and social appearance—still raised questions. However, this was a critical step toward simplifying the profile from multiple individuals to feIr.

In our analysis of the eyewitness accounts, I noticed that headgear played a significant role in the descriptions of the suspect. Two specific types of hats caught our attention: the *deerstalker* and the *peaked cloth cap*. At first, I grouped them together with some caution, due to some similarities. However, upon closer examination, it became clear that while they share certain features, they are not the same and should be treated as distinct entities.

The Deerstalker Hat vs. Peaked Cloth Cap

Deerstalker Hat: This is a distinctive hat with two brims—one in the front and one in the back—often associated with countryside attire and famously worn by Sherlock Holmes. It's typically made of cloth, such as tweed, and has ear flaps that can be tied on top or under the chin. The shape is unique, making it an unusual choice for an urban environment like Whitechapel, but its description in multiple eyewitness accounts suggests that it was a memorable feature.

Peaked Cloth Cap: This is a simpler, more common hat with a single brim or peak at the front, often worn by sailors or working-class individuals in the late 19th century. It does not have the dual brim or ear flaps seen in the deerstalker. This style was widespread in Whitechapel, particularly among laborers, which made it a plausible headgear for the suspect.

Initial Grouping: In Joseph Lawende's description of a man at the scene of Catherine Eddowes' murder, the reference to a *peaked cloth cap* seemed to fit into our emerging profile of the suspect. At first, I grouped this with the deerstalker sightings due to the similarity of having a front peak, but after careful review, it became evident that these hats, while both peaked, were distinct in style. Thus, they should not be merged unless there is strong contextual support indicating a similar look.

Felt Hat Confusion: Deerstalker or Just Felt?

Another point of consideration was the possibility of confusion between a *felt hat* and a *deerstalker*. Although a deerstalker is traditionally made of cloth materials like tweed, felt is a common hat material and could potentially have been used in the construction of a deerstalker. This opened the door to some ambiguity in eyewitness reports, especially under poor lighting or stressful conditions.

Possible Confusion: A witness might focus on the material (felt) rather than the specific style (deerstalker) if they only got a brief or partial glimpse of the suspect. Additionally, from certain angles, a deerstalker could resemble a single-brimmed felt hat, particularly if the observer was unfamiliar with the distinct dual-brim shape of the deerstalker. Thus, I considered merging some of the felt hat descriptions with deerstalker mentions, though I remained cautious of the differences.

Merging of Descriptions: Disregarding Shaving and Age

As part of my synthesis of the descriptions, I also considered that certain details—such as facial hair and age—could vary significantly depending on lighting and the suspect's ability to alter his appearance between sightings. Shaving, for example, could easily change between events, while age is often difficult to estimate accurately, particularly in poor light conditions. Therefore, I decided to disregard these factors when evaluating the overall consistency of the descriptions.

For example, let us take the following eyewitness descriptions:

- **Emily Walter (Annie Chapman, 2:00 A.M.)**: Black felt hat, foreigner, dark beard and moustache, dark jacket, vest, trousers.

- **Elizabeth Long (Annie Chapman, 5:30 A.M.)**: Brown deerstalker hat, dark complexion, possibly a dark overcoat, foreigner.

- **P.C. William Smith (Elizabeth Stride, 12:30 A.M.)**: Hard dark felt deerstalker hat, dark clothes, clean-shaven, aged 28, respectable.

- **James Brown (Elizabeth Stride, 12:45 A.M.)**: Long black diagonal coat, 5'7", stout, felt hat (not explicitly deerstalker but felt).

By focusing on the headgear, clothing, and general appearance rather than factors like facial hair and age, which could easily be altered or misjudged, I was able to group these descriptions with moderate confidence.

Considering Height and Agreement Between Descriptions

Another factor I examined was the height discrepancy. While some witnesses described the suspect as 5'7", others placed him closer to 5'4". Given the conditions under which these descriptions Ire made—often at night and from a distance—I agreed that these height ranges could reasonably be merged.

Height: Once I merged the height descriptions into a range of 5'4" to 5'7", I found greater agreement between the accounts.

Hat: Three out of four descriptions mention a felt or deerstalker hat, creating some agreement on headwear, though the specific type (deerstalker vs. felt) differs slightly.

Complexion: Both Emily Walter and Elizabeth Long mention a dark complexion, though the other accounts do not specify.

Clothing: Three descriptions mention dark clothing, with some additional details like a long black coat or vest. This creates reasonable consistency across the witnesses.

Conclusion on Merging

On a Likert scale, the level of agreement between these four descriptions can be rated as moderate to good. While there are some inconsistencies, particularly regarding facial hair and age, the significant overlaps in headgear, dark clothing, and height suggest that these witnesses may have observed the same individual. The possibility of confusion between a felt hat and a deerstalker, especially under challenging observation conditions, adds to this likelihood. This process of merging descriptions helped simplify our profile of the suspect and brought us closer to a coherent understanding.

After removing the clusters that I previously merged based on shared characteristics—such as the presence of a deerstalker hat or dark felt hat—I was left with a handful of descriptions that had yet to be analyzed in detail. These included the account by Joseph Lawende, which had initially been set aside due to its reference to a peaked cloth cap, as Ill as several other key eyewitness reports.

In this chapter, I take a fresh look at these remaining descriptions to explore whether they form new clusters or provide further insights into the suspect's identity. Below is a table of the remaining eyewitness accounts:

CHAPTER 4. MY ANALYSIS

Witness	Description
Matthew Packer (Elizabeth Stride, 12:00–12:30 A.M.)	Aged 25-30, 5'7", long black coat buttoned up, soft felt hat, broad shoulders. Possibly a young clerk, frock coat, no gloves.
Israel Schwartz (Elizabeth Stride, 12:45 A.M.)	First man: Aged 30, 5'5", brown-haired, fair complexion, small brown moustache, full face, broad shoulders, dark jacket and trousers, black cap with a peak. Second man: Aged 35, 5'11", fresh complexion, light brown hair, dark overcoat, old black hard felt hat with a wide brim, clay pipe.
Joseph Lawende (Catherine Eddowes, 1:30 A.M.)	Aged 30, 5'7", fair complexion, brown moustache, salt-and-pepper coat, red neckerchief, grey peaked cloth cap. Sailor-like appearance.
Mary Ann Cox (Mary Kelly, 11:45 P.M.)	Short, stout man, shabbily dressed, billycock hat, blotchy face, carroty moustache, holding a quart can of beer.
George Hutchinson (Mary Kelly, 2:00 A.M.)	Aged 34-35, 5'6", pale complexion, dark hair, slight moustache curled at each end. Long dark coat, light waistcoat, gold chain, dark trousers, gaiters, red kerchief, respectable Jewish appearance.

With these descriptions in hand, I now begin the process of clustering and analyzing them based on their commonalities, differences, and any potential for confusion or overlap.

Clustering the Remaining Descriptions

Our approach to clustering this time focused on the key distinguishing factors, such as clothing (especially outerwear), height, facial hair, and headgear. This allowed us to create two distinct clusters from the remaining descriptions.

Cluster 1: Long Coats and Broad Shoulders

This cluster includes individuals with long coats and broad shoulders, along with similar age and height ranges:

- **Matthew Packer (12:00–12:30 A.M., Elizabeth Stride Scene)**: Aged 25-30, 5'7", long black coat buttoned up, soft felt hat, broad shoulders, possibly a young clerk.

- **Joseph Lawende (1:30 A.M., Catherine Eddowes Scene)**: Aged 30, 5'7", fair complexion, brown moustache, salt-and-pepper coat, red neckerchief, grey peaked cloth cap.

- **George Hutchinson (2:00 A.M., Mary Kelly Scene)**: Aged 34-35, 5'6", pale complexion, dark hair, slight moustache curled at each end, long dark coat, respectable Jewish appearance.

Agreement in Cluster 1:

- *Clothing:* All three men are described as wearing long dark coats, suggesting a commonality in outerwear.

- *Headgear:* The headgear varies slightly between soft felt hats and peaked cloth caps, but the hats are all dark and somewhat formal, fitting the description of men who might be trying to maintain a respectable appearance.

- *Facial Hair:* All have moustaches, with Hutchinson's being more distinct (curled at each end), while Lawende and Packer describe more typical facial hair.

- *Height:* The height ranges from 5'6" to 5'7", which aligns closely enough to consider these individuals as potentially the same.

The consistency in long coats, facial hair, and respectable appearance across this cluster suggests that these descriptions could refer to the same person or individuals with similar attire and physical features.

Cluster 2: Felt Hats and Dark Clothing

The second cluster groups together men who wore felt hats or dark clothing but differ somewhat in build and appearance:

- **Israel Schwartz (12:45 A.M., Elizabeth Stride Scene):**
    - First man: Aged 30, 5'5", brown-haired, fair complexion, small brown moustache, broad shoulders, dark jacket and trousers, black cap with a peak.
    - Second man: Aged 35, 5'11", fresh complexion, light brown hair, dark overcoat, old black hard felt hat with a wide brim, clay pipe.

- **Mary Ann Cox (11:45 P.M., Mary Kelly Scene):** Short, stout man, shabbily dressed, billycock hat, blotchy face, carroty moustache, holding a quart can of beer.

Agreement in Cluster 2:

- *Clothing:* Dark clothing appears in all three descriptions, though there's more variety in outerwear (dark jacket, dark overcoat, shabbily dressed).

- *Headgear:* Hats are present in all sightings, though they vary significantly (black peaked cap, hard felt hat, billycock hat).

- *Facial Hair:* All three men have moustaches, though their styles and colors differ (brown, light brown, carroty).

- *Height:* The height ranges are wider in this cluster, from 5'5" to 5'11", and Mary Ann Cox's man is explicitly described as short and stout, distinguishing him from the others.

This cluster is more varied, especially when it comes to height and the overall appearance of the men. However, the commonality of dark clothing and headgear ties them together, and the presence of moustaches helps maintain some consistency across the descriptions.

Considering Lawende's Sighting

One notable inclusion in this phase of the analysis is the account by Joseph Lawende, who described a man near the scene of Catherine Eddowes' murder wearing a peaked cloth cap and sailor-like clothing. At first, this sighting was set aside due to the difference in headgear, but upon further consideration, it was reintroduced due to the similarity in height, facial hair, and overall build when compared to the other descriptions in Cluster 1. The peaked cloth cap, while distinct from the deerstalker and felt hats seen elsewhere, shares enough of a working-class, practical aesthetic to warrant inclusion in this grouping.

Agreement Across the Remaining Descriptions

Finally, by clustering these remaining descriptions, I can assess the overall level of agreement:

Hat/HeadIar: Moderate agreement. The hats described are varied, but most descriptions include dark or felt materials, and all are practical for the period and setting.

Complexion: Good agreement. Most descriptions feature fair to pale complexions, though Mary Ann Cox's description of a "blotchy face" stands out as an exception.

Clothing: Very good agreement. Long dark coats or dark clothing are a common theme across both clusters.

Facial Hair: Good agreement. All witnesses describe moustaches, though the color and style vary.

Height: Moderate agreement. Most witnesses describe heights between 5'5" and 5'7", though Israel Schwartz's second man and Mary Ann Cox's man deviate from this range.

In summary, this phase of the analysis revealed moderate to good agreement between the remaining descriptions, allowing us to further refine the suspect's profile.

After our thorough analysis and clustering process, it became increasingly clear that while I managed to merge some descriptions based on similarities in clothing, facial hair, and headgear, I Ire still faced with the realization that the eyewitness accounts might still refer to as many as five or six distinct men. The hope that these accounts could describe a single individual seemed to fade as I delved deeper into the details. Below, I revisit the final clusters and reflect on the implications of these findings.

Cluster 1: "Dark Coat and Felt Hat Men"

This cluster groups together individuals with dark coats and felt hats, but despite the apparent similarities, the minor differences (e.g., facial hair, build) and the time gaps suggest that I may still be dealing with multiple men:

- **Emily Walter (2:00 A.M., Annie Chapman Scene)**: Black felt hat, dark beard, dark clothing, foreigner.

- **Elizabeth Long (5:30 A.M., Annie Chapman Scene)**: Brown deerstalker hat, dark complexion, dark overcoat, foreigner.

- **P.C. William Smith (12:30 A.M., Elizabeth Stride Scene)**: Dark felt deerstalker hat, dark clothes, cleanshaven.

- **Matthew Packer (12:00–12:30 A.M., Elizabeth Stride Scene)**: Soft felt hat, long black coat.

Conclusion: Despite the commonality in clothing (dark coats and felt hats), the distinctions in facial hair (beard vs. cleanshaven) and the timing of the sightings suggest that these descriptions could be referring to **2 or 3 distinct men**.

Cluster 2: "Structured Hat and Respectable Appearance"

This cluster brings together individuals who Ire described with more structured hats (peaked or turned-down hats) and had a generally respectable appearance. However, the slight variations in hat styles and other details leave room for interpretation:

- **Joseph Lawende (1:30 A.M., Catherine Eddowes Scene)**: Grey peaked cloth cap, sailor-like, long coat.
- **George Hutchinson (2:00 A.M., Mary Kelly Scene)**: Dark hat, turned down in the middle, long coat, respectable, Jewish appearance.

Conclusion: These sightings likely describe **1 or 2 distinct men**. The differences in headgear (peaked cloth cap vs. turned-down hat) suggest two different individuals, but the overall respectable appearance and long coats make some overlap possible.

Cluster 3: "Shabby, Stout Men"

This cluster includes descriptions of men who Ire noted for their stout, shabby appearance, along with similar descriptions of hats:

- **Mary Ann Cox (11:45 P.M., Mary Kelly Scene)**: Billycock hat, short, stout, shabbily dressed, blotchy face.
- **James Brown (12:45 A.M., Elizabeth Stride Scene)**: Felt hat, stout, long black diagonal coat.

Conclusion: These two sightings most likely describe **1 distinct man**, given the strong agreement in physical build (stout) and the shabby appearance.

Cluster 4: "Distinct Men from Israel Schwartz's Sighting"

Finally, I come to Israel Schwartz's account, which clearly describes two distinct men seen in the same location around the same time. These two men are described with enough detail to rule out any overlap between them:

- **First Man (12:45 A.M., Elizabeth Stride Scene)**: Brown-haired, fair complexion, small brown moustache, black cap.

- **Second Man (12:45 A.M., Elizabeth Stride Scene)**: Fresh complexion, light brown hair, dark overcoat, old black felt hat, light brown hair, clay pipe.

Conclusion: This account likely describes **2 distinct men**, given the clear differences in appearance and behavior described by Israel Schwartz.

Final Estimate: Five to Six Distinct Men

After this round of clustering and analysis, it became clear that despite our best efforts to consolidate descriptions, the eyewitness reports most likely refer to **five or six distinct men**. While some descriptions share significant overlap—particularly regarding clothing and headgear—the variations in height, facial hair, and build, along with the timing of the sightings, make it hard to reduce this number further.

Unifying the Clusters: The Emerging Profile of Jack the Ripper

Our analysis began with a seemingly insurmountable challenge: reconciling the disparate eyewitness descriptions of men seen near the scenes of the Whitechapel murders. Initially, the details painted a picture of multiple individuals—a dark-bearded foreigner here, a stout man with a carroty mustache there, and even the polished figure described by George Hutchinson. Yet, as we systematically revisited the testimonies, patterns began to emerge.

The first step was to revisit the issue of the mustache. Some witnesses described a "brown mustache," while others noted it as "carroty." Initially, this distinction had seemed significant, but on closer examination, it became less persuasive. Under gaslight or in the dim streets of Whitechapel, brown and reddish-brown facial hair could easily be interpreted differently by multiple observers. These mustaches were, in all likelihood, describing the same feature. By collapsing this distinction, we brought together sightings of a man with a broad-shouldered build and facial hair into a single, more consistent group.

Next came the testimony of George Hutchinson. His detailed description of a well-dressed, astrakhan-clad man stood in stark contrast to every other account. His testimony—offered days after the fact—was rich in detail to a degree that raised suspicion. Most witnesses described men in dark, workaday clothing, unremarkable in their appearance. Hutchinson's suspect was a glaring outlier. Removing this account—recognizing it as likely exaggerated or fabricated—brought the remaining testimonies into sharper focus.

Lastly, there was the sighting of the man with the beer. Mary Ann Cox's account of a stout, blotchy-faced man carrying a quart of beer to Mary Jane Kelly's room initially appeared too mundane to warrant much attention. But within the larger analysis, this man stood out as more significant. His stout build, carroty mustache, and billycock hat aligned with other descriptions of broad-shouldered, rough-looking men. More importantly, his behavior suggested something darker—a man attempting to intoxicate his victim, a small but critical hint of manipulation. Restoring him to the analysis added coherence to the emerging profile.

By applying a logical, step-by-step process, we arrived at a unified suspect profile. Key decisions in this synthesis included:

- Treating **brown and carroty mustaches** as effectively the same feature. Given the stress, poor lighting, and brief encounters under which these descriptions were made, minor variations in color could reasonably be attributed to perceptual differences rather than actual discrepancies.

- **Disregarding George Hutchinson's testimony.** His elaborate account of a well-dressed, astrakhan-clad man stands in stark contrast to every other description. Hutchinson's sudden willingness to provide such a detailed narrative—days after the murder—has long raised suspicions of fabrication, likely for attention or other motives.

- **Restoring the man with the beer** from Mary Ann Cox's sighting. Initially sidelined as an outlier, this man, described as stout, blotchy-faced, with a carroty mustache and billycock hat, fits well within the broader pattern of a manipulative, working-class figure. His behavior—holding a quart of beer, potentially to intoxicate Mary Jane Kelly—aligns disturbingly with the predator's modus operandi.

The Revised Clusters

With these adjustments, the previous clusters collapse into a far simpler and more cohesive structure. What once appeared to describe five or six individuals now converges into two distinct clusters that ultimately point to a single, unified suspect.

Cluster 1: Stout Men in Dark Coats and Felt Hats These descriptions feature men with stout builds, dark coats, and various forms of felt headwear—deerstalker, billycock, or soft felt hats. The commonalities in appearance far outweigh their minor differences.

- **Matthew Packer's man** (Elizabeth Stride, 12:00–12:30 A.M.): Soft felt hat, long black coat, broad shoulders.

- **P.C. William Smith's man** (Elizabeth Stride, 12:30 A.M.): Dark felt deerstalker hat, dark clothes, clean-shaven, respectable.

- **James Brown's man** (Elizabeth Stride, 12:45 A.M.): Stout build, long black diagonal coat, felt hat.

- **Mary Ann Cox's man** (Mary Kelly, 11:45 P.M.): Billycock hat, stout, blotchy face, carroty mustache, carrying beer.

Cluster 2: Men with Brown or Carroty Mustaches, Broad Shoulders Descriptions from multiple witnesses highlight facial hair as a distinguishing feature—specifically, a brown or carroty mustache—and the presence of broad shoulders, often paired with dark clothing.

- **Israel Schwartz's first man** (Elizabeth Stride, 12:45 A.M.): Small brown mustache, broad shoulders, dark jacket and trousers, black cap.

- **Mary Ann Cox's man** (Mary Kelly, 11:45 P.M.): Carroty mustache, broad shoulders, stout build, dark clothing.

Convergence of the Clusters

At this point, the distinctions between Cluster 1 and Cluster 2 begin to blur. Both describe:

- A **stout, broad-shouldered man**, consistently seen wearing dark, working-class clothing—whether a long black coat, dark trousers, or both.

- A man with a **brown or carroty mustache**, a recurring detail across witnesses.

- Headgear that, while varying slightly (billycock, soft felt, or deerstalker), shares the commonality of being dark, felt-based, and practical for late-night movement in cold, damp Whitechapel streets.

The inconsistencies—such as facial hair, precise hat style, or slight variations in height—can be attributed to the conditions under which the sightings occurred. Poor lighting, brief glimpses, and the unreliable nature of memory in high-stress situations likely account for these minor discrepancies. By focusing on the shared traits, the broader patterns become undeniable.

The Unified Profile of Jack the Ripper

Our analysis now points toward a single, unified suspect:

> A stout, broad-shouldered man, standing approximately 5'5" to 5'7", of working-class appearance, wearing dark, durable clothing—a long black coat or jacket—and a dark felt hat, variously described as a billycock, soft felt, or deerstalker. He had a brown or carroty mustache and a rough, unremarkable demeanor that allowed him to blend seamlessly into the streets of Whitechapel. His behavior suggests a manipulative streak, exemplified by the man carrying beer, who may have been attempting to gain Mary Jane Kelly's trust before her murder.

Figure 4.1: AI-generated image of the suspect.

This figure is not the flamboyant, aristocratic killer of conspiracy theories, nor the spectral, faceless villain that mythologized versions of the Ripper often portray. Instead, he is a far more chilling presence—an ordinary man, unassuming yet deadly, who used the anonymity of his working-class appearance to move unseen through the fog-laden streets. He was both everywhere and nowhere, lurking in plain sight.

To further clarify the suspect profile that has emerged, an image was generated using AI based on the consolidated description. The resulting visual captures the key traits described by multiple witnesses: a stout, broad-shouldered man, wearing dark working-class clothing, a long coat, and a felt hat, with a brown or carroty mustache. While this representation is speculative, it serves as a useful tool for conceptualizing the figure who moved unseen through Whitechapel's streets.

Chapter 5

Known Suspects Through a New Lens

Having distilled the eyewitness accounts into a coherent description of one man—stout and broad-shouldered, around 5'5" to 5'7" in height, wearing dark working-class clothing and a felt hat, with a brown or carroty mustache—we must now consider how this profile aligns with the known suspects in the case. This exercise may help us determine whether any of the traditionally suspected individuals truly fits the picture that has emerged from our analysis. Before we compare our consolidated description to specific suspects, let us first review the major candidates who have been proposed over the years:

The Traditional Suspects

Aaron Kosminski emerged as a prime suspect through the investigations of Sir Robert Anderson and Chief Inspector Donald Swanson. A Polish Jew living in Whitechapel, Kosminski was known to suffer from mental illness and was eventually institutionalized. The case against him gained renewed attention in recent years due to contested DNA evidence supposedly linking him to a shawl found at one of the crime scenes.

Montague John Druitt, a barrister and schoolteacher, came under suspicion largely due to the timing of his suicide in December 1888, shortly after the last canonical murder. His death by drowning in the Thames, combined with family suggestions of mental instability, has kept him in the spotlight of Ripper investigations for over a century.

George Chapman, born Seweryn Kłosowski, worked as a barber in Whitechapel during the time of the murders. He was later convicted and hanged for poisoning three of his wives, showing a clear capacity for calculated murder, albeit through different means than the Ripper's brutal knife work.

Charles Allen Lechmere, also known as Charles Cross, has gained attention in recent years due to his discovery of Polly Nichols' body and his suspicious behavior afterward. His work as a cart driver gave him legitimate reason to be in the area of the murders at various hours.

Francis Tumblety, an American quack doctor, was arrested in London for unrelated crimes during the Ripper's reign of terror. His documented hatred of women, particularly prostitutes, and his subsequent flight to America have kept him under consideration.

Michael Ostrog, a Russian-born con artist and thief, made the list of suspects primarily due to his criminal background and presence in London during the relevant period. However, little concrete evidence links him to the murders.

CHAPTER 5. KNOWN SUSPECTS THROUGH A NEW LENS

The following is a ranked comparison of the suspects using the revised profile:

1. George Chapman (Seweryn Kłosowski)

Physical Description: Chapman's build was described as stout and broad-shouldered, closely aligning with the physical description settled on during our analysis. While his facial hair was typically recorded as brown, it remains consistent with the descriptions of a brown or carroty mustache.
Height: Chapman was reportedly around 5'5" to 5'7", perfectly fitting the consolidated height profile.
Clothing: As a barber working in Whitechapel at the time, Chapman would have worn dark, practical clothing befitting a respectable working-class tradesman.
Behavior: Chapman's later crimes—poisoning three wives—reveal a calculated and manipulative streak, albeit a departure from the overt violence seen in the Ripper murders. However, his ability to lure victims and evade suspicion speaks to a pattern of control and predation.
Similarity Score: Very Good.

Chapman's physical description, attire, and location in Whitechapel align strongly with our refined profile, though his later methods of killing deviate from the Ripper's.

2. Charles Allen Lechmere (Charles Cross)

Physical Description: Lechmere's exact height is not well-documented, but he is widely assumed to have been between 5'5" and 5'7", which aligns with the eyewitness accounts. As a cart driver, his profession would have contributed to a stout, broad-shouldered build.
Clothing: Lechmere's occupation required functional, dark clothing, typical of the working-class attire repeatedly noted by witnesses.
Behavior: Lechmere's proximity to the murder of Polly Nichols and his inconsistent statements to the police place him under suspicion. As a cart driver, he had reason to move through Whitechapel at odd hours, making his presence near the crime scenes less conspicuous.
Similarity Score: Very Good.

Lechmere fits the physical, occupational, and behavioral aspects of the refined profile, presenting a plausible explanation for his movements during the murders.

3. Aaron Kosminski

Physical Description: Kosminski was reported as thin and frail—traits that directly conflict with the stout, broad-shouldered figure repeatedly described by witnesses.
Height: Kosminski's height is poorly documented, but no reports suggest he matched the average height described by the witnesses.
Clothing: Kosminski, being impoverished and mentally ill, likely wore tattered or disheveled clothing rather than the dark, respectable working-class attire described.
Behavior: While Kosminski's deteriorating mental health eventually led to his institutionalization, there is little evidence to suggest manipulative behavior or an ability to lure victims.
Similarity Score: Poor.

Despite his significance in historical investigations, Kosminski does not align with the consolidated profile's physical description or behavioral traits.

4. Montague John Druitt

Physical Description: Druitt was described as tall and slender, which stands in stark contrast to the stout, broad-shouldered man consistently seen by witnesses.
Height: At approximately 6 feet tall, Druitt far exceeds the height range described in our profile.
Clothing: Druitt came from an upper-class background and likely wore formal clothing inconsistent with the dark, working-class attire noted by witnesses.
Behavior: Druitt's suicide shortly after the final canonical murder and his family's claims of mental instability have kept him under suspicion, but his physical appearance eliminates him as a strong match.
Similarity Score: Very Poor.

Druitt's build, height, and class position make him an unlikely fit for the profile emerging from the eyewitness descriptions.

5. Francis Tumblety

Physical Description: Tumblety was reportedly tall and well-built, conflicting with the shorter, stout figure described by witnesses.
Height: Tumblety's height—over 6 feet—places him far outside the consolidated range of 5'5" to 5'7".
Clothing: Tumblety was known for his flamboyant and extravagant attire, which is entirely at odds with the dark, working-class clothing seen by witnesses.
Behavior: Tumblety's documented misogyny and hatred of prostitutes align with the psychological profile of the Ripper, but his physical appearance and eccentric clothing are significant points of contradiction.
Similarity Score: Poor.

While Tumblety fits certain behavioral aspects of the Ripper, his height and flamboyant attire make him an unlikely match.

6. Michael Ostrog

Physical Description: Ostrog's height and build are poorly documented, leaving his physical alignment with the profile unclear. However, there is no evidence suggesting he was stout or broad-shouldered.
Clothing: As a career criminal and con artist, Ostrog likely adapted his appearance as needed. However, no accounts suggest that he wore the consistent, dark working-class attire described by witnesses.
Behavior: Ostrog's criminal background makes him a plausible manipulator, but there is little evidence connecting him directly to the Ripper murders.
Similarity Score: Moderate.

While Ostrog's history as a criminal is relevant, his physical traits and lack of proximity to the murders make him a weaker match for the refined profile.

Final Reranking of Suspects

1. **George Chapman (Seweryn Kłosowski)** – Very Good
2. **Charles Allen Lechmere (Charles Cross)** – Very Good
3. **Michael Ostrog** – Moderate
4. **Aaron Kosminski** – Poor
5. **Francis Tumblety** – Poor
6. **Montague John Druitt** – Very Poor

Focusing on the Visual Match

While earlier analysis incorporated both physical traits and behavioral evidence, it is worthwhile to also consider an analsyis in which only the visual elements reported by witnesses stand as the closest thing to primary, unbiased evidence.

Hence, we evaluate, ignoring behavioral speculation, how well do the known suspects match the physical description we have built—a stout, broad-shouldered man, standing around 5'5" to 5'7", wearing dark, working-class clothing, a felt hat (such as a billycock or deerstalker), and possibly with a brown or carroty mustache?

Focusing purely on the visual profile allows us to strip away narrative layers that history has imposed on these suspects. This approach ensures we are guided only by what witnesses saw and reported in the immediate aftermath of the murders. Below, I evaluate the primary suspects on visual characteristics alone.

The Visual Comparison

1. George Chapman (Seweryn Kłosowski) **Height:** Chapman stood around 5'5" to 5'7", precisely matching the height range described by witnesses.
Build: Chapman was described as stout and broad-shouldered, a strong match for the consolidated profile.
Clothing: As a barber in Whitechapel, Chapman likely wore dark, practical working-class attire.
Facial Hair: He was known to have a brown mustache, aligning closely with witness accounts of facial hair.
Visual Match: Excellent.

Chapman aligns remarkably well with the consolidated visual profile on all significant traits: height, build, clothing, and facial hair.

2. Charles Allen Lechmere (Charles Cross) **Height:** Though Lechmere's exact height is not documented, most accounts place him at an average build, likely within the 5'5" to 5'7" range.
Build: As a cart driver, Lechmere's profession would have given him a stout, broad-shouldered physique, matching the visual profile.
Clothing: Lechmere's working-class background would have ensured he wore dark, durable clothing, consistent with witness accounts.
Facial Hair: No definitive record of Lechmere's facial hair exists, which leaves this point

uncertain.
Visual Match: Very Good.

Lechmere fits almost all aspects of the profile except for the lack of clarity regarding his facial hair.

3. Aaron Kosminski   Height: Kosminski was described as thin and frail, which contradicts the stout, broad-shouldered figure consistently reported by witnesses.
Build: His slender build does not align with the profile.
Clothing: Kosminski, living in poverty and suffering from mental illness, likely wore tattered and unremarkable clothing—not the dark, respectable working-class attire noted in descriptions.
Facial Hair: Kosminski is often described as cleanshaven, with no evidence of a prominent mustache.
Visual Match: Very Poor.

Kosminski's physical description fails to match the consolidated visual traits in almost every category.

4. Montague John Druitt   Height: Druitt's tall stature—around 6 feet—places him well outside the 5'5" to 5'7" range.
Build: Druitt was slender, not stout, further contradicting the profile.
Clothing: Druitt's middle-class background suggests formal attire that does not match the dark, working-class clothing consistently described by witnesses.
Facial Hair: There is no record of Druitt having a mustache.
Visual Match: Very Poor.

Druitt's tall, slender build and upper-class background make him a poor fit for the visual description.

5. Francis Tumblety   Height: Tumblety's height—well over 6 feet—does not match the consolidated range.
Build: While Tumblety was well-built, his extreme height makes him an unlikely match.
Clothing: Tumblety's known penchant for flamboyant, eccentric clothing directly contradicts the descriptions of dark, practical working-class attire.
Facial Hair: Tumblety had a mustache, but this alone does not overcome the discrepancies in other traits.
Visual Match: Poor.

Tumblety's height and clothing style place him far outside the boundaries of the visual profile.

6. Michael Ostrog   Height: Ostrog's height is poorly documented, making it difficult to assess against the profile.
Build: There is little evidence to suggest that Ostrog had the stout, broad-shouldered build described by witnesses.
Clothing: As a career criminal, Ostrog may have adapted his attire to various circumstances, though there is no strong evidence linking him to the consistent working-class clothing described.
Facial Hair: There is no clear record of Ostrog's facial hair.
Visual Match: Moderate.

While Ostrog remains a weak contender in terms of physical traits, his adaptable appearance prevents him from being ruled out entirely.

Final Ranking: Purely Visual Matches

1. **George Chapman (Seweryn Kłosowski)** – Excellent
   Chapman matches the height, build, clothing, and facial hair described with remarkable consistency.

2. **Charles Allen Lechmere (Charles Cross)** – Very Good
   Lechmere aligns well with the height, build, and clothing, though uncertainty remains about his facial hair.

3. **Michael Ostrog** – Moderate
   Ostrog lacks strong evidence aligning with the visual profile but cannot be entirely dismissed.

4. **Francis Tumblety** – Poor
   Tumblety's extreme height and flamboyant clothing clash with the eyewitness descriptions.

5. **Aaron Kosminski** – Very Poor
   Kosminski's thin, frail build and likely tattered clothing fail to match any significant aspect of the profile.

6. **Montague John Druitt** – Very Poor
   Druitt's tall, slender frame and upper-class attire stand in stark contrast to the stout, working-class man described by witnesses.

Adding Psychological Profiling and Writing Ability to the Analysis

While matching the visual descriptions alone brought us closer to understanding the man described by witnesses, the analysis remains incomplete without considering additional elements of the case. The psychological profiling conducted by the FBI gives us a behavioral framework to compare against known suspects, while the ability to write the infamous Ripper letters adds another layer of comparison. Combined, these three elements—*visual description*, *FBI profiling*, and *writing ability*—allow for a more robust evaluation of the primary suspects.

The FBI Psychological Profile

The FBI psychological profile of Jack the Ripper provides critical insights into the likely personality and background of the killer:

1. The Ripper would be a white male.
2. Between 25 and 35 years old.
3. Lived locally to the Whitechapel/Spitalfields area.

4. A loner, likely unmarried.

5. Raised by a dominant mother figure, with an absent father.

6. A mental or physical disability or deformity, which made him feel different from others.

7. Worked a solitary job, limiting his social interactions.

8. Perceived as quiet, timid, and odd by those who knew him.

9. Beneath the surface would lie a deep, resentful aggression, which would explode during bouts of low self-esteem.

10. He would lack guilt or remorse for his crimes, potentially justifying them in his mind.

Matching the Suspects: Visual Description and FBI Profile

To refine our analysis further, we now focus solely on two vectors for comparison: the *visual descriptions* provided by witnesses and the *FBI psychological profile* of Jack the Ripper. By disregarding the letter-writing ability entirely, we strip away any speculative distractions and anchor the evaluation purely to appearance and behavioral characteristics.

This approach ensures that our conclusions are driven by the most concrete and consistent elements of the case: what witnesses reported seeing and what modern behavioral science tells us about the likely traits of the killer.

The Reranked Suspects

1. George Chapman (Seweryn Kłosowski) **Visual Description:** Chapman matches the stout, broad-shouldered physical build described by witnesses. His height (approximately 5'5" to 5'7") aligns closely with the range noted in the eyewitness accounts. As a barber, he wore dark, working-class clothing consistent with the descriptions. **FBI Profile:** Chapman fits many elements of the FBI psychological profile:

- He was white and in his early 30s during the murders.

- He lived locally in Whitechapel, working as a barber-surgeon.

- His later crimes—poisoning his wives—demonstrate a deep-seated resentment and a capacity for calculated violence.

- While he was married, his misogynistic tendencies align with the Ripper's likely psychological characteristics.

Conclusion: Chapman is an excellent match for both the visual description and the psychological profile.

CHAPTER 5. KNOWN SUSPECTS THROUGH A NEW LENS

2. Charles Allen Lechmere (Charles Cross) Visual Description: Lechmere closely aligns with the visual profile. He was of average height (believed to be around 5'5" to 5'7"), stout, and dressed in dark, functional working-class clothing as part of his work as a cart driver. **FBI Profile:**

- Lechmere was white, lived locally in Whitechapel, and worked a solitary job that required him to move through the streets at odd hours.
- He was in his late 30s, which places him slightly older than the FBI's suggested range but still within plausible limits.
- Described as quiet and ordinary, Lechmere fits the profile of someone perceived as unremarkable but harboring potential latent aggression.

Conclusion: Lechmere is a very strong match, with his physical traits and solitary working-class job aligning well with both vectors.

3. Jacob Levy Visual Description: Levy, as a butcher, had a stout, strong build and was of average height, around 5'3" to 5'5". While slightly shorter than the witness descriptions, he fits the general physical profile reasonably well. **FBI Profile:**

- Levy was a white male, in his early 30s, and lived locally in Whitechapel.
- His work as a butcher was solitary and provided him with anatomical knowledge consistent with the Ripper's mutilations.
- Levy's deteriorating mental health, which led to his institutionalization, aligns with the profile of someone feeling different or alienated from others.

Conclusion: Levy is a good match, particularly for his build, local presence, and solitary occupation.

4. Aaron Kosminski Visual Description: Kosminski's thin, frail build contradicts the stout, broad-shouldered descriptions of the Ripper. His height was also likely below the 5'5" to 5'7" range, making him a weaker visual match. **FBI Profile:**

- Kosminski was a white male, in his mid-20s, living in Whitechapel at the time of the murders.
- His severe mental illness and reclusive nature align with the FBI's image of a loner who felt different from others.
- However, his frailty and lack of documented violence weaken his alignment with the profile of someone harboring explosive aggression.

Conclusion: Kosminski fits key elements of the FBI profile but does not align with the visual descriptions.

CHAPTER 5. KNOWN SUSPECTS THROUGH A NEW LENS

5. David Cohen / Nathan Kaminsky **Visual Description:** Cohen was described as physically strong and violent, aligning with the stout figure described by witnesses. However, his severe mental illness complicated this alignment, as his frailty due to institutionalization weakens his match. **FBI Profile:**

- Cohen/Kaminsky were white males living locally in Whitechapel.
- Their mental instability fits the profile of someone who felt alienated from society.
- However, their extreme mental deterioration likely made them incapable of carrying out such precise and calculated murders.

Conclusion: Cohen and Kaminsky match some elements of the profile but lack consistency in both physical traits and controlled behavior.

6. Henry Tomkins **Visual Description:** Tomkins, a horse slaughterer, was described as rough-looking and of low stature. While his physical description aligns with a stout, working-class figure, his shorter height weakens his overall match. **FBI Profile:**

- Tomkins lived locally and worked a solitary, physical job that matches the FBI projection.
- There is little evidence, however, of the deep psychological aggression or alienation described in the profile.

Conclusion: Tomkins fits visually but lacks sufficient psychological alignment with the FBI profile.

7. Montague John Druitt **Visual Description:** Druitt was tall and slender, which directly conflicts with the stout, broad-shouldered descriptions. **FBI Profile:**

- Druitt was not a local resident of Whitechapel and came from a middle-class background, which clashes with the profile of a local, working-class killer.
- There is no strong evidence of the resentment or low self-esteem projected in the FBI profile.

Conclusion: Druitt fails to align with both the visual and psychological profiles.

8. Francis Tumblety **Visual Description:** Tumblety was over six feet tall, flamboyantly dressed, and well-built—traits that are inconsistent with the stout, working-class descriptions provided by witnesses. **FBI Profile:**

- Tumblety's hatred of women aligns with the FBI projection of deep, resentful aggression.
- However, his status as an aristocratic outsider does not match the profile of a local, lower-class resident.

Conclusion: Tumblety matches the psychological aggression but fails in visual traits and local connection.

CHAPTER 5. KNOWN SUSPECTS THROUGH A NEW LENS   49

9. Prince Albert Victor **Visual Description:** Prince Albert Victor, as royalty, was tall, aristocratic, and entirely inconsistent with the visual description of the Ripper. **FBI Profile:** The profile strongly indicates someone of lower-class origins living locally. Prince Albert fails entirely to meet these characteristics. **Conclusion:** Albert does not match either the visual or psychological profile.

10. Joseph Merrick (The Elephant Man) **Visual Description:** Merrick's severe deformities make him a poor match for the stout, broad-shouldered figure described by witnesses. **FBI Profile:** Though Merrick may have felt alienated, his physical limitations prevent him from matching the traits of the calculated and controlled killer described by the FBI. **Conclusion:** Merrick does not align with either vector.

11. Lewis Carroll **Visual Description:** Carroll's slight, intellectual build fails to align with the stout, working-class descriptions of Jack the Ripper. **FBI Profile:** Carroll, as a reclusive upper-class figure, does not match the local, psychologically aggressive traits outlined in the profile. **Conclusion:** Carroll is an extremely poor match.

Final Ranking Based on Visual and FBI Profile

1. **George Chapman (Seweryn Kłosowski)** – Excellent
2. **Charles Allen Lechmere (Charles Cross)** – Very Good
3. **Jacob Levy** – Good
4. **Aaron Kosminski** – Moderate
5. **David Cohen/Nathan Kaminsky** – Moderate
6. **Henry Tomkins** – Moderate
7. **Montague John Druitt** – Moderate
8. **Francis Tumblety** – Moderate
9. **Prince Albert Victor** – Very Poor
10. **Joseph Merrick** – Very Poor
11. **Lewis Carroll** – Very Poor

Chapter 6

The Most Compelling Match

Over the course of this investigation, one suspect has consistently emerged as an especially credible contender for the identity of Jack the Ripper: George Chapman, born Seweryn Kłosowski. While historical mysteries rarely yield absolute certainties, the striking convergence of Chapman's documented appearance, locations, skills, and subsequent criminal behavior suggests a closer alignment with the contemporary eyewitness accounts than any other known individual.

Chapman's story begins in Poland, where he trained as a field doctor—an experience that would later resonate with certain aspects of the Whitechapel murders. After immigrating to London, he settled into a modest profession as a barber in the East End. This profession, however, belied a certain cosmopolitan adaptability; by contemporary accounts, he cultivated a "shabby genteel" demeanor, fluidly navigating between working-class milieus and more genteel circles. In other words, Chapman epitomized a man who could alter his appearance and manner to suit circumstance, a chameleon-like ability that would have benefited a predator operating within Whitechapel's dense and diverse community.

This duality is vividly captured in surviving photographs. Chapman, though not well-off, presented himself as a man of style and self-regard. He favored neatly tailored suits, a carefully curled mustache, fashionable floral lapel adornments, and a thick gold watch chain. Such sartorial details align with George Hutchinson's description of the man last seen with Mary Jane Kelly, and yet Chapman also maintained the capacity to blend seamlessly into the working-class environment where he plied his trade. In this manner, he could appear, as different witnesses reported, both as a "shabby genteel" foreigner and as a more respectably dressed figure about town.

Physical Correspondences

The known physical attributes of George Chapman bear a remarkable resemblance to the composite descriptions drawn from multiple witness accounts. Standing approximately 5'6" to 5'7", he matched the stature consistently recorded in testimonies. His physique, reputedly stout and broad-shouldered, aligns closely with several contemporary descriptions.

More striking still is the careful attention Chapman paid to grooming. He wore his mustache curled at the ends—just as George Hutchinson noted—and often sported a flower in his lapel, mirroring the detail observed by PC Smith regarding the man seen with Elizabeth Stride. Chapman's mastery of varying his appearance adds further weight to these correspondences. Though known for wearing stylish dark suits, he could also present himself in a more modest, even seaman-like guise, sporting both sailor caps and felt hats. This eclectic wardrobe elegantly resolves previously perplexing contradictions in witness statements, which seemed to describe multiple individuals rather than one man adept at changing his look.

Geographical Connections and Local Knowledge

Chapman's geographical footprint during the Ripper murders situates him squarely within the killer's operational theater. His barbershop at 126 Cable Street was only a short walk from Berner Street, where Elizabeth Stride was murdered, placing him in proximity to one of the crime scenes. His daily routines, social connections, and occupational ties would have furnished him with detailed knowledge of local streets, alleys, and escape routes—an invaluable advantage for anyone seeking to evade detection.

Moreover, Chapman's earlier lodgings at 70 West India Dock Road connected him to an area closely linked to the initial attacks on women like Emma Smith. Familiar with both the labyrinthine streets of Whitechapel and the dynamic rhythms of dockside life, Chapman stood at the nexus of local geography and sociability. His barbershop, a community hub, allowed him to monitor police activities and neighborhood chatter from behind an unremarkable veneer of everyday commerce.

Professional Skills and Capabilities

Perhaps the most compelling element of Chapman's profile is his medical background. Trained as a field doctor in Poland, he possessed anatomical knowledge far beyond that of an ordinary laborer. The Ripper murders, which demonstrated surgical precision and a clear understanding of human anatomy, strongly suggest a perpetrator with at least a rudimentary medical background. Chapman's education placed him in precisely that category.

Additionally, as a Victorian barber, Chapman would have been adept at handling razors and other sharp instruments, not to mention performing basic surgical procedures. These dual competencies—formal medical training and daily familiarity with blades—would have equipped him with both the technical skill and manual dexterity to inflict the lethal, targeted wounds reported in the Ripper murders. His professional environment also provided easy access to disguise materials, such as wigs and hair dyes, potentially facilitating swift changes in appearance that could have confounded witnesses and investigators.

The Evolution of Violence

Caution is warranted when connecting disparate crimes to a single individual, yet Chapman's subsequent history of violence cannot be ignored. His murder of women by poisoning in later years demonstrates a willingness, even an aptitude, for deliberate and methodical homicide. While the Ripper's brutal, disfiguring acts differ from the more surreptitious killings Chapman eventually committed, criminal psychologists acknowledge that killers can alter their methods over time. Adaptation might reflect the increasing

CHAPTER 6. THE MOST COMPELLING MATCH

sophistication of a perpetrator who, having learned from past risks, switches to less detectible methods of murder.

Contemporary parallels, such as the attack on Mary Ann Austin in Dorset Street, highlight disturbing continuities in Chapman's presence and potential involvement. Although it is impossible to state definitively that Chapman was responsible for all or any of the Whitechapel murders, the alignment of pattern, presence, and skillset is nonetheless unsettling.

Assessing the Cumulative Weight of Evidence

The case for Chapman as a prime Ripper suspect rests upon a substantial body of circumstantial evidence:

- **Physical Appearance:**
    - Matches witnesses' reported height and build
    - Sporting a curled mustache, as per Hutchinson's testimony
    - The capacity to appear both respectable and "shabby genteel," fitting various testimonies
    - Wearing flowers in his lapel and favoring multiple hat styles, echoing key eyewitness details

    vbnet Copy code

- **Location and Timing:**
    - Lived and worked near all key murder sites
    - His barbershop on Cable Street aligned closely with the scene of Stride's murder
    - Familiarity with dockland environs correlates with earlier victim sightings

- **Professional Expertise:**
    - Medical training likely provided anatomical knowledge reflected in the murders
    - Barbering skills ensured comfort with sharp implements and delicate procedures
    - Ready access to disguise materials explains the fluidity in reported appearances

Counterpoints and Considerations

As compelling as the Chapman hypothesis may be, it is not without caveats:

- His later pivot to poisoning represents a stark methodological shift.
- No definitive physical evidence links Chapman to the Ripper crimes.
- The maintenance of a stable business and social life during the murder series raises questions about whether he could sustain such extreme violence undetected.

Conclusion

George Chapman emerges as perhaps the closest known match to the Ripper based on the evidence currently available. His documented attributes, professional background, geographic positioning, and proven capacity for calculated murder place him squarely among the most plausible suspects. The endorsement of Inspector Abberline—who had direct and intimate knowledge of the original investigation—further underlines the credibility of this candidacy.

Nevertheless, the absence of conclusive, material proof and the inherent limitations of historical data mean we must remain circumspect. The identity of Jack the Ripper may never be definitively established. Still, based on the alignment of eyewitness testimony, geographic familiarity, medical skill, and subsequent criminal activities, George Chapman stands as the suspect who most convincingly embodies the elusive figure who haunted the streets of Whitechapel in 1888.

In sum, while Chapman's guilt cannot be conclusively proven, the weight of circumstantial evidence suggests that in George Chapman we may have found the individual who came closest to fitting both the description and modus operandi of the Whitechapel murderer. As with so many facets of the Ripper legend, absolute certainty remains beyond our grasp, but the case for Chapman remains notably stronger than that for any other known suspect.

Chapter 7

Final Thoughts: The Power of Primary Evidence

As we conclude this investigation into one of history's most enduring mysteries, it's worth reflecting on what we've learned through our data-driven approach to the Jack the Ripper case. By returning to the primary evidence—the eyewitness accounts taken immediately after the murders—and analyzing them through the lens of modern data analysis and psychological profiling, we've uncovered patterns that previous investigators may have overlooked.

Our journey began with what appeared to be an insurmountable challenge: reconciling seemingly contradictory eyewitness descriptions that had frustrated researchers for over a century. The initial examination of these accounts suggested we were looking at five or six different men, which aligned with the traditional view that these testimonies were unreliable or inconsistent. However, by applying systematic analysis and pattern recognition, we discovered that these apparently disparate descriptions could be consolidated into a remarkably coherent profile of a single individual.

The key to this breakthrough lay in our methodology. Rather than dismissing accounts that didn't immediately align, we looked for underlying patterns and considered how factors such as lighting conditions, stress, and the killer's ability to modify his appearance might have influenced witness perceptions. This approach revealed that many of the supposed contradictions in witness statements could be reconciled when viewed through the lens of a single suspect who could adapt his appearance while maintaining certain consistent physical characteristics.

Our analysis yielded a specific profile: a stout, broad-shouldered man of average height (5'5" to 5'7"), typically wearing dark, working-class clothing and various styles of felt hats, including a deerstalker. This man possessed a brown or carroty mustache and could present himself anywhere on the spectrum from "shabby genteel" to respectably dressed. This ability to modify his appearance while maintaining core physical characteristics explains why witnesses sometimes described him differently, yet with consistent underlying features.

When we compared this profile against known suspects, one individual emerged as a remarkably close match: George Chapman (Seweryn Kłosowski). Chapman's documented physical characteristics, occupation, and presence in Whitechapel aligned strikingly well with our consolidated witness descriptions. His background as a barber-surgeon provided him with both the anatomical knowledge and comfort with sharp implements that the murders demonstrated. His proven capacity for calculated murder, albeit through different means in later years, adds weight to his candidacy.

However, it's crucial to acknowledge the limitations of our investigation. While the evidence points compellingly toward Chapman, we cannot claim absolute certainty. The passage of time, the loss of physical evidence, and the inherent limitations of historical investigation mean that the true identity of Jack the Ripper may never be known with complete certainty. What we can say is that our data-driven approach has identified the suspect who best fits the available evidence.

The significance of this investigation extends beyond simply pointing to a likely suspect. It demonstrates the value of returning to primary sources and applying modern analytical techniques to historical mysteries. By stripping away layers of speculation and focusing on contemporary witness accounts, we've shown how seemingly contradictory evidence can reveal coherent patterns when examined systematically.

This methodology also challenges some common assumptions about the Ripper case. The killer wasn't necessarily the aristocratic figure of popular imagination, nor was he likely to be the deranged madman often portrayed in media. Instead, the evidence suggests a more mundane but perhaps more chilling reality: a calculating predator who could blend seamlessly into the fabric of Whitechapel society, hiding his murderous nature behind a facade of respectability.

The lessons learned from this investigation have implications for both historical research and criminal investigation. They remind us that witness testimony, often dismissed as unreliable, can contain valuable insights when analyzed properly. They also demonstrate how preconceptions and later speculation can obscure rather than illuminate historical truth.

As we close this examination, we must remember that behind the analytical discussion lie real victims whose lives were brutally ended. Mary Ann Nichols, Annie Chapman, Elizabeth Stride, Catherine Eddowes, and Mary Jane Kelly were more than just names in a historical case file. They were women struggling to survive in the harsh environment of Victorian London, and their murders deserve to be understood as more than just elements of a mystery.

While this investigation has brought us closer to understanding who Jack the Ripper might have been, it also serves as a reminder of how difficult it is to achieve absolute certainty in historical cases. Yet through careful analysis of primary evidence and the application of modern analytical techniques, we can come closer to the truth than ever before. The solution to the Ripper mystery may not lie in sensational theories or conspiracy scenarios, but in the methodical examination of what witnesses saw and reported in those dark autumn nights of 1888.

The story of Jack the Ripper continues to captivate us not just because of its mysterious nature, but because it represents a pivotal moment in the history of crime and investigation. By applying modern analytical techniques to this historical case, we've demonstrated how new approaches can shed light on old mysteries. While we may never know with absolute certainty who Jack the Ripper was, we can now say with greater confidence than ever before who he most likely was, and how he managed to terrorize Whitechapel while hiding in plain sight.

Printed in Dunstable, United Kingdom